Windsor Ontario Book 3 in Colour Photos, Saving Our History One Photo at a Time

I0469781

Photography
by Barbara Raué
2015

Series Name:
Cruising Ontario

Book 119: Windsor Book 3 –

Including Sandwich Village, the whiskey business,
and shots of Detroit Michigan

Cover photo: Hiram Walker Main Office Building (Page 24)

Series Name: Cruising Ontario
Saving Our History One Photo at a Time in colour photos

Books Available in Alphabetical Order:
Aberfoyle, Acton, Alton, Ancaster, Arthur, Aylmer, Ayr, Bloomingdale, Brantford, Burlington, Caledon, Caledonia, Cambridge, Clifford, Conestogo, Delhi, Dorchester to Aylmer, Drayton, Drumbo, Dundas, Eden Mills, Elmira, Elora, Fergus, Guelph, Hagersville, Hamilton, Hanover, Harriston, Hespeler, Jarvis, Kitchener, Linwood, Listowel, London, Lucknow, Mono, Mount Forest, Neustadt, New Hamburg, Niagara-on-the-Lake, Oakville, Orangeville, Orillia, Owen Sound, Palmerston, Peterborough, Port Elgin, Preston, Rockwood, Seaforth, Sheffield, Shelburne, Simcoe, Southampton, St. Jacobs, St. Thomas, Stoney Creek, Stratford, Tillsonburg, Waterdown, Waterrford, Waterloo, Wellesley, Wingham

Book 110:Lucknow,Mitchell
Book 111: Conestogo, Bloomingdale
Book 112: Delhi
Book 113: Waterford
Book 114-116: Waterloo
Book 117-119: Windsor

Other Books by Barbara Raue

Coins of Gold

Arrows, Indians and Love

The Life and Times of Barbara
Volume 1: Inventions That Have Enhanced My Life
Volume 2: Entertainment That I Have Enjoyed
Volume 3: East Coast Trips
Volume 4: Olympics Have Always Intrigued Me
Volume 5: Wonders of the World
Volume 6: Caribbean Cruises We Have Enjoyed
Volume 7: Animals
Volume 8: Storms and Other Major Disasters in My Lifetime
Volume 9: Wars, Terrorist Attacks and Major Disasters

The Cromwell Family Book

Laura Secord Discovered

Daddy Where Are You?

Visit Barbara's website to view all of her books
http://barbararaue.ca

Windsor is the southernmost city in Canada. The Detroit River is to the north of the city, which separates it from Detroit, Michigan. Windsor was settled by the French in 1749 as an agricultural settlement. In 1794, after the American Revolution, the settlement of "Sandwich" was founded. It was later renamed Windsor, after the town in Berkshire, England.

On July 12, 1812, Brigadier-General William Hull, Commander of the North Western Army of the United States, landed with about 2,000 men near the site of the Hiram Walker main office building. He issued a proclamation stating that he came to liberate Canada from oppression. The British garrison at Amherstburg was too weak to oppose the invasion but later fought several skirmishes at the River Canard. On July 26, British reinforcements under Colonel Henry Procter arrived and on August 7-8, Hull withdrew to Detroit leaving a small garrison near Sandwich which retired on August 11 at the approach of Major-General Isaac Brock.

Sandwich, Ford City and Walkerville were separate towns until 1935 when they were annexed by Windsor. They remain as historic neighbourhoods of Windsor. Sandwich was established in 1817 as a French agricultural settlement; it was incorporated as a town in 1858.

The Sandwich neighbourhood on Windsor's west side is home to some of the oldest buildings in the city, including Mackenzie Hall, originally built as the Essex County Courthouse in 1855. Today, this building functions as a community centre. The City of Windsor was the site of the Battle of Windsor during the Upper Canada Rebellion in 1838. It was also a part of the Patriot War later that year.

The Underground Railroad is neither a railroad nor is it underground. It is the name of the network of people who hid and guided slaves and refugees as they followed the North Star to Canada to freedom. From 1440 to the late 1800s, millions of Black Africans were shipped under primitive conditions to the Americas to service the sugar plantation industry. Less than 15 million survived the middle passage and because of harsh living conditions and extreme cruelty in their new homeland, many more died from disease and exhaustion. The Underground Railroad movement originated in the southern United States and wound its way to the less restricted North and eventually stretched to Canada.

Windsor is the headquarters of Hiram Walker & Sons Limited, now owned by Pernod Ricard. Its historic distillery was founded by Hiram Walker in 1858 in what was then Walkerville. During the 1920s alcohol prohibition was enforced in Michigan while alcohol was legal in Ontario. Rum-running in Windsor was a common practice during that time period.

Table of Contents

Hiram Walker

Hiram Walker was born in East Douglas, Massachusetts, and moved to Detroit in 1838. In 1847 at the age of 30, he married Mary Abigail Williams and they had seven children, two daughters, Julia Elizabeth and Jennie Melissa, and five sons, Willis Ephraim, Edward Chandler, Franklin Hiram, Alfred (infant), and James Harrington. Edward Chandler, his second son, commissioned the development of Willistead Manor.

He was an American entrepreneur and he purchased 460 acres of land across the Detroit River in the town of Sandwich, near Windsor, Ontario, Canada. In 1858 the flour mill and distillery were completed. The flour produced in his mill benefited the County of Essex's farming community with farmers from all around using the mill.

Mid-summer in 1858 marked the opening of Hiram Walker's whisky operation. The same process which he had used in Detroit was now used in Windsor to distill his alcohol. Spirits were leached through charcoal, a process widely used at the time. Walker began selling his whisky as Hiram Walker's Club Whisky and it became very popular. His Canadian industries quickly took precedent over that of his grain business still located in Detroit. As a result, Hiram Walker travelled by ferry to Canada from his home in Detroit on a daily basis. The trip was a lengthy process as the ferry that brought him to Canada dropped him off in Windsor, which left a long ride by horse and buggy to his flour mill and distillery. Throughout his life, Hiram Walker remained an American citizen but in March 1859 Hiram Walker moved to Canada in order to save time traveling to and from his Canadian businesses. For a period of five years until 1864, he lived in Windsor in a residence named the "Cottage" which was on land that was part of the Labadie holdings which

Hiram originally purchased and was located near the flour mill. The "Cottage" was a home previously owned by the Labadie family from whom Hiram Walker had purchased much of the land his industries were located on. This framed house was built in 1839 and resembled the French style of residences prevalent in the area. Walker made several modifications to the home including two large additions at each end of the home, and the addition of a third floor as well as a servants' dwelling.

Hiram's business created an expansion of the town that included malt houses, cooperage, copper shop, planning mill, lumber yard, brick yard, and a ferry between Walkerville and Detroit. Walker decided to invest in a ferry that would travel between Detroit and Walkerville to save time. He installed a dock system on his land in Walkerville that allowed people to board the ferry and a set schedule was developed in 1881 and the ferry as a public service began with the ferry called "Ariel."

Hiram Walker built a railroad that extended from Walkerville to the outskirts of Kingsville, a distance of twenty-seven miles. Walker established and maintained the company town that grew around his distillery, exercising planning and control over every facet of the town, from public works to religious services to police and fire control. The new industries and people in Walkerville because of these transportation opportunities led to the creation of good roads that could sustain heavy traffic, traffic lights, police and firemen, and proper sanitary measures. All of these necessities for a town to properly function could not be afforded by the rural municipality of Sandwich East (what Walkerville was called before its official name) so Hiram Walker and Son's funded everything, including water, fifty-two firemen, the fire appliances, two police officers who rotated shifts, repairs of streets and sidewalks, the night watch service, the electric lighting of the streets, the Music Hall, the Anglican Church, and even some privately owned houses. Hiram's efforts to make Walkerville a legitimate town led to his title as Walkerville's mayor. Hiram created a town council that included the mayor, councilors, clerks, treasurers, medical health officers, collectors, assessors, auditors, solicitors, and the chief of police and policeman.

The popularity of his whisky angered American distillers who forced the U.S. government to pass a law requiring that all foreign whiskeys state their country of origin on the label. From this point forward, Hiram Walker's famous Canadian Club Whisky was Canada's top export whisky.

The Hiram Walker & Sons Distillery remained in the Walker family until 1926 when they sold it to Harry C. Hatch. Canadian Club Whisky is still produced at the distillery site Walker founded.

In 1859, Walker hired John McBride to be his travelling salesman, one of his workers from Detroit. His job was to travel and solicit orders from vendors interested in purchasing the product. The year 1860 was of the highest production because both his mill and distillery were running almost non-stop.

Hiram Walker is recognized as the man who gave momentum to such aspects that benefited the community as trading, agricultural work, stock raising, building industries, and most importantly, inspired those who saw his perseverance and progressive attitudes. Hiram built homes for his employees and rented them out at reasonable prices, and he created public utilities, paved the streets, and paid for and encouraged people to get an education. Walker erected a Methodist church in 1870 which was converted into an Anglican Church in 1874, and renamed St. Mary's in honour of Walker's late wife, Mary.

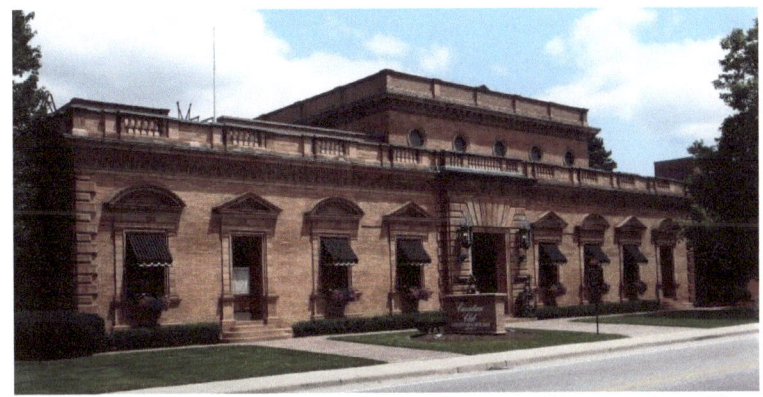

2072 Riverside Drive East – Hiram Walker main office building 1894 – Florentine Renaissance

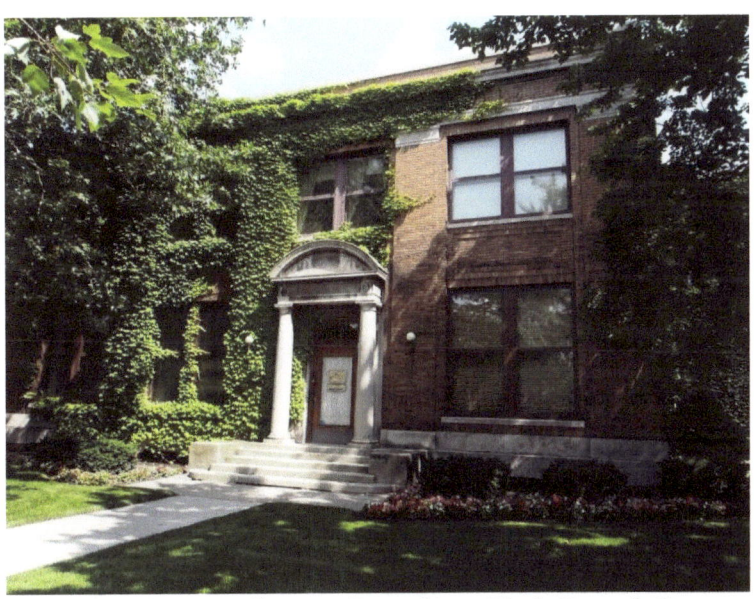

Walkerville Distillery – Canadian Club Brand Center since 1858

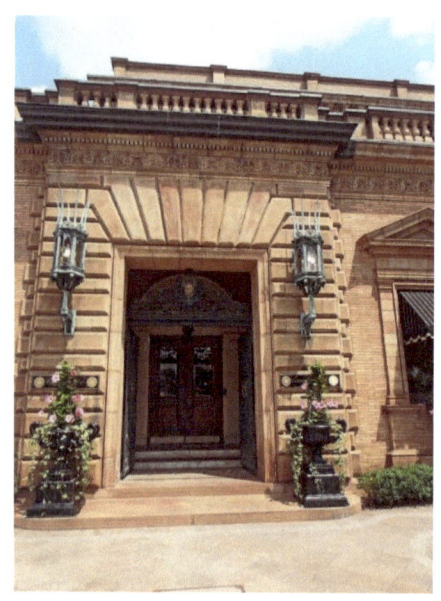

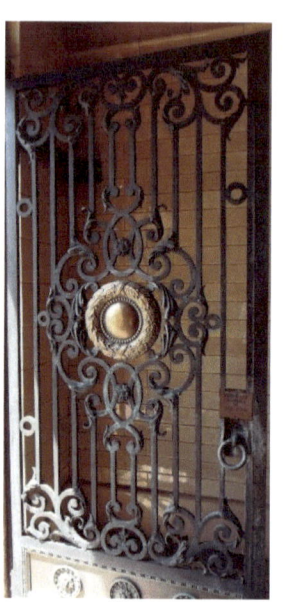

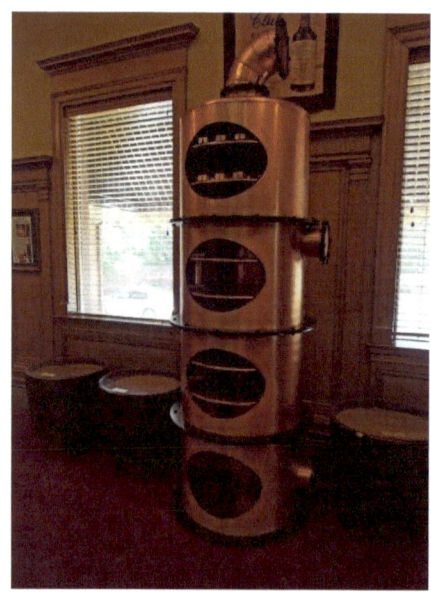

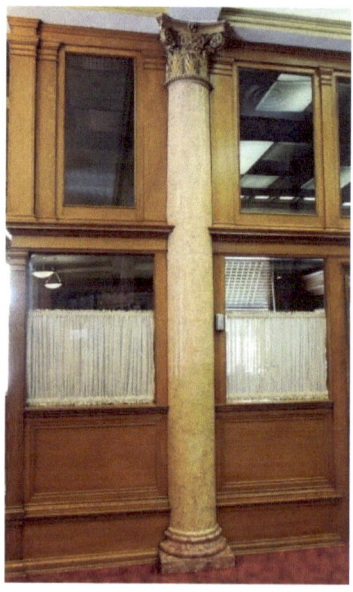

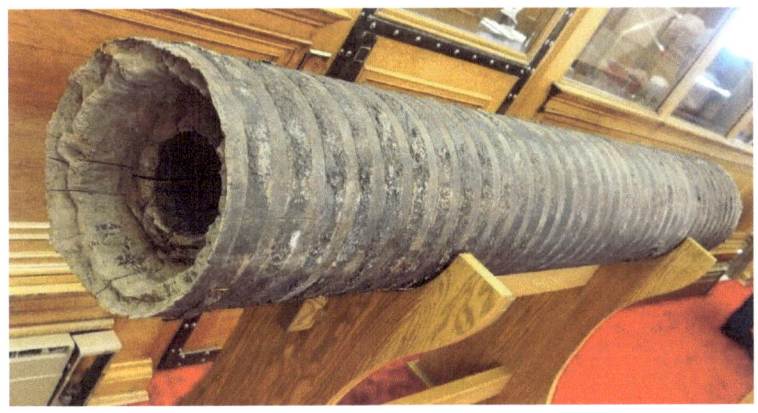

Bored out cypress log was a small section of the mile-long underground piping system that pumped distillers mash to the Walker cattle farms at the intersection of Walker Road and Tecumseh Road East. Buried for almost 120 years, the excellent condition of this pipe is testament to the high quality of materials and craftsmanship that characterized Hiram Walker's ventures. Distillers spent mash (with the alcohol removed) was used to fatten Walker's cattle for domestic and international markets.

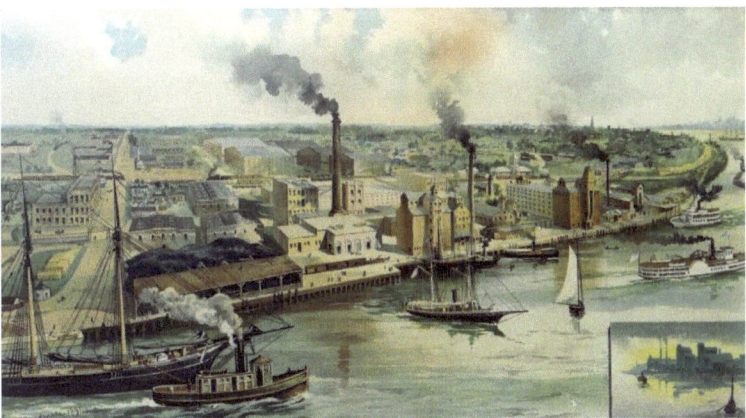

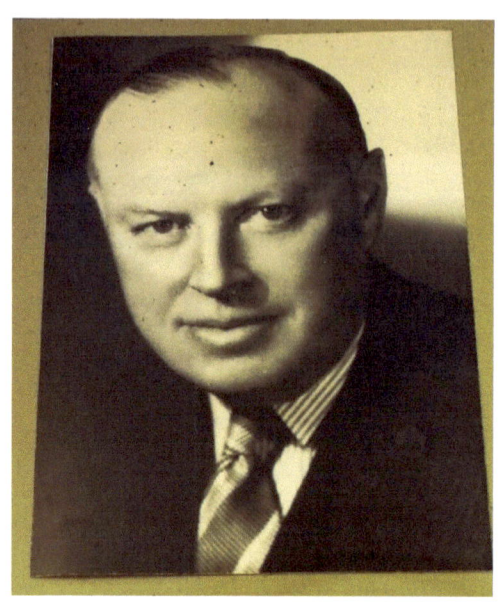

Harry C. Hatch was born in Ameliasburg, Prince Edward County, and went to school in Deseronto. For a time he worked with his father in the hotel business. In 1911 he bought a liquor store in Whitby for $2,500 and sold it two years later for $14,000. He moved to Toronto with his brother in 1913 and opened another liquor store. In 1916, prohibition came along and they were faced with heavy losses. Two days after prohibition's arrival, he was in business in Montreal, serving his Toronto customers by mail order. The business became enormously successful. He purchased the Gooderham & Worts Distillery in Toronto in 1923 for $1,000,000 and three years later took over the Hiram Walker Distillery, paying $15,000,000. The two companies were merged and became Hiram Walker Gooderham & Worts, one of the largest distilleries in the world. For the next five decades under the Hatch family leadership the company enjoyed spectacular growth and prosperity.

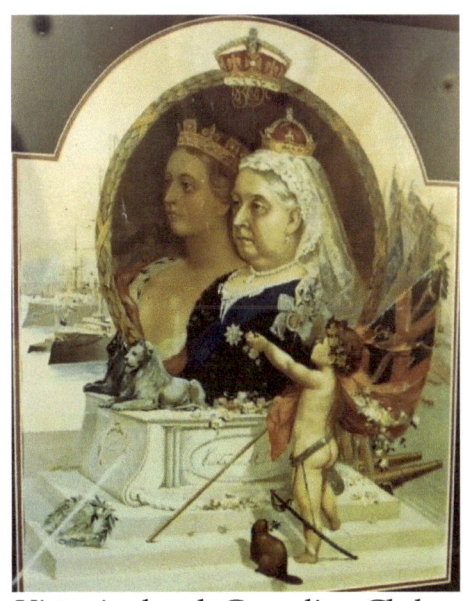

Queen Victoria drank Canadian Club whiskey
The Royal Warrant, the coat of arms of the reigning British
monarch, is granted to firms that have supplied goods directly
to the royal household for at least three years. The Royal
Warrant was first granted to Hiram Walker & Sons Limited by
Queen Victoria in 1898. Since the death of Queen Victoria, the
Royal Warrant has been granted to Hiram Walker by Edward
VII, George V, George VI, and Queen Elizabeth II.

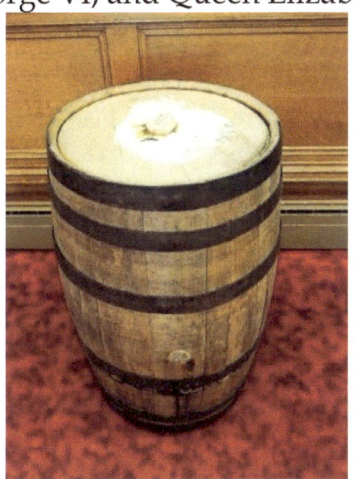

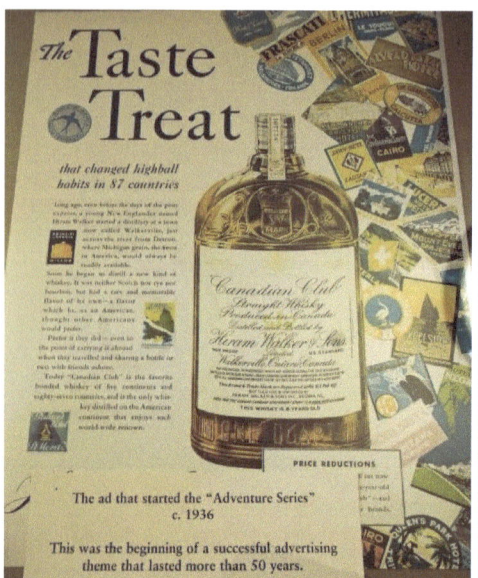

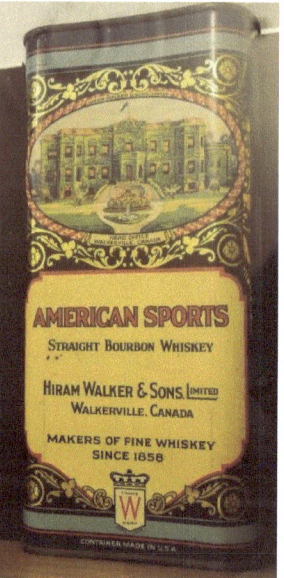

The Ad that started the "Adventure Series" c. 1936 was the beginning of a successful advertising theme that lasted for more than fifty years.

At midnight January 16, 1920 saloons and taverns throughout the United States closed. This was the climax to a fifty year campaign to eliminate the use of liquor. What U.S. Prohibition did was to create speakeasies, flappers, rumrunners, and colourful personalities. In Canada it was perfectly legal to produce and sell alcohol, and as a result, most of the whiskey sold in the United States was made in Canada and smuggled across the border.

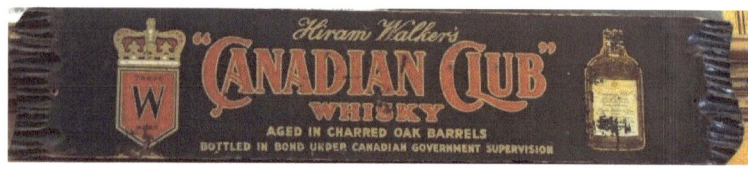

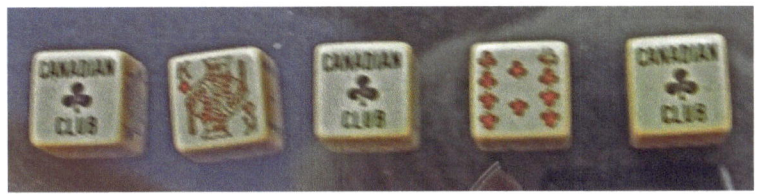

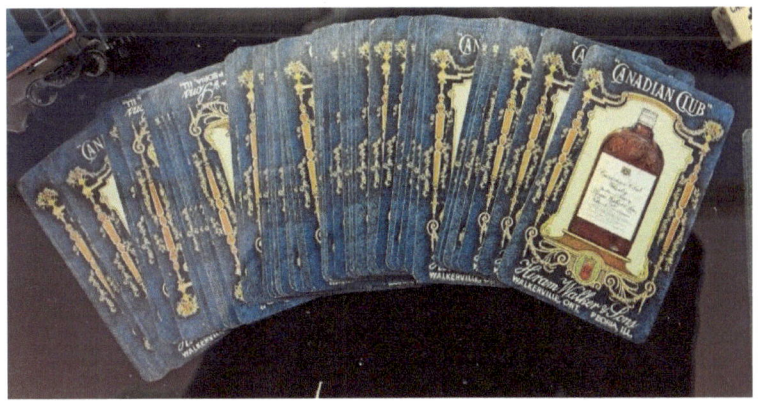

Canadian Club Whiskey dice and playing cards

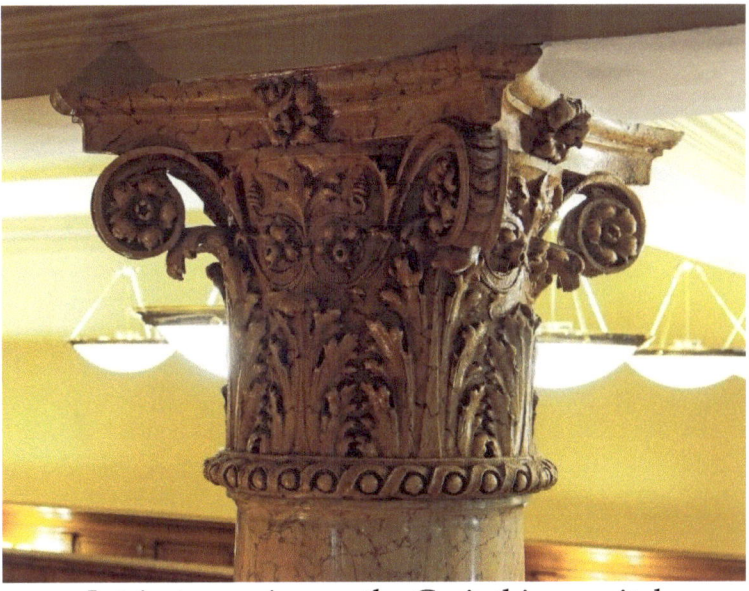

Intricate carving on the Corinthian capital

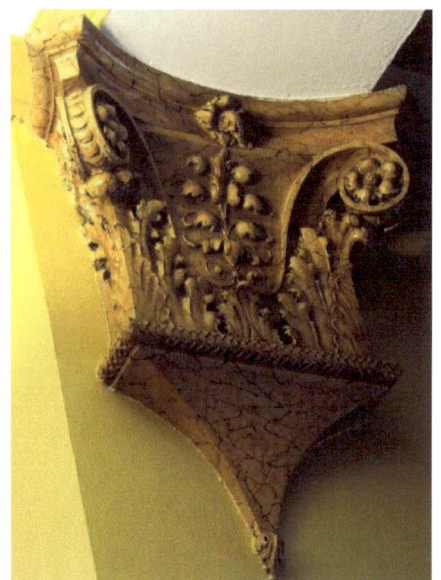
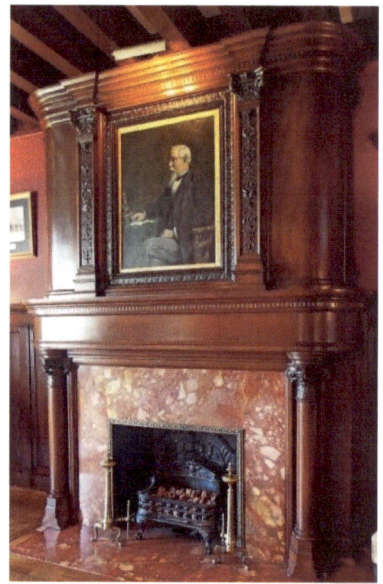

Marble on fireplace from Egypt in Hiram's office

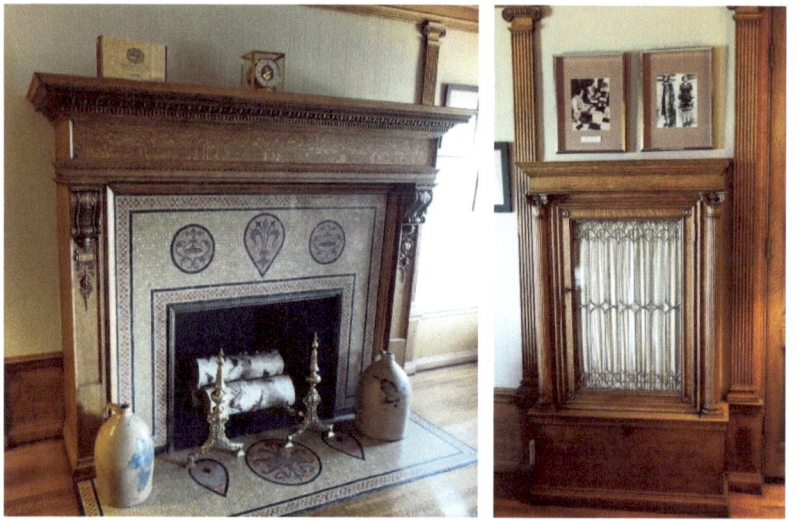

Son Edward's office – Edward was responsible for building the first Ford plant in Walkerville in 1904 to manufacture and selling the cars in Canada and the British Empire. It was originally known as the Walkerville Wagon Works, was located in Walkerville. The Ford cars were used during the winter to cross the Detroit River with liquor.

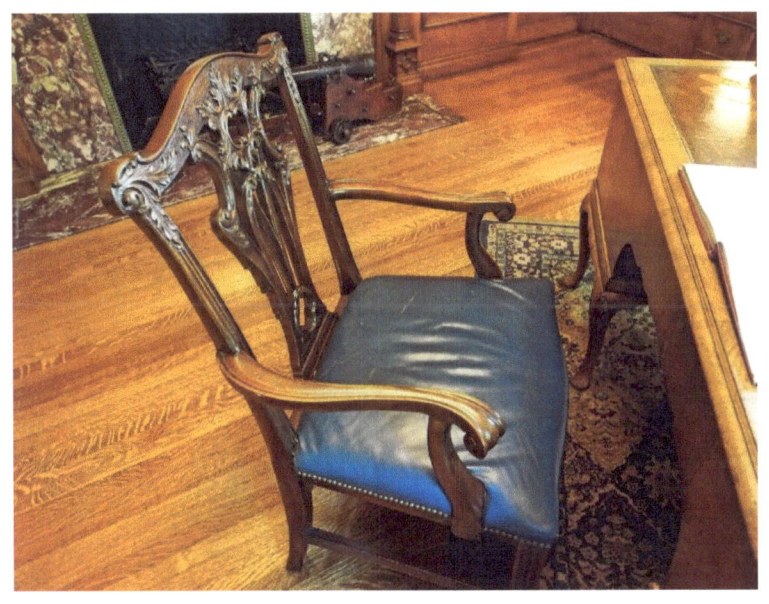

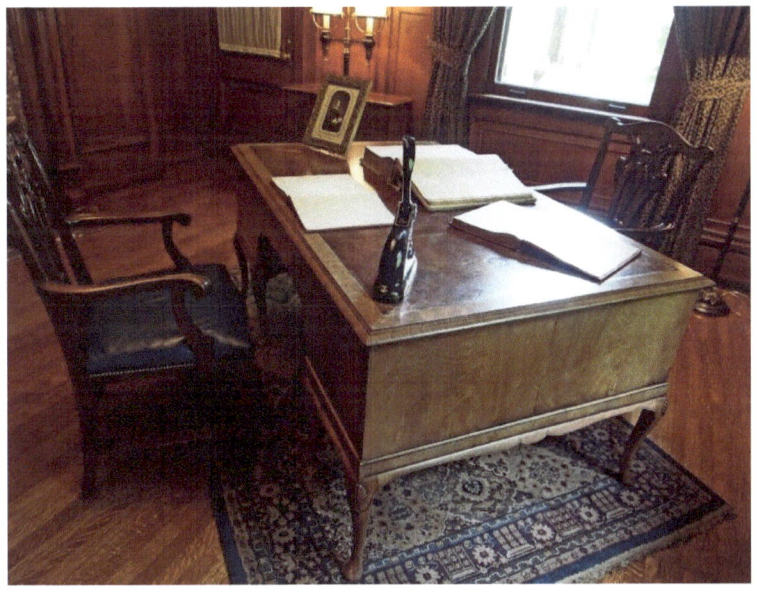

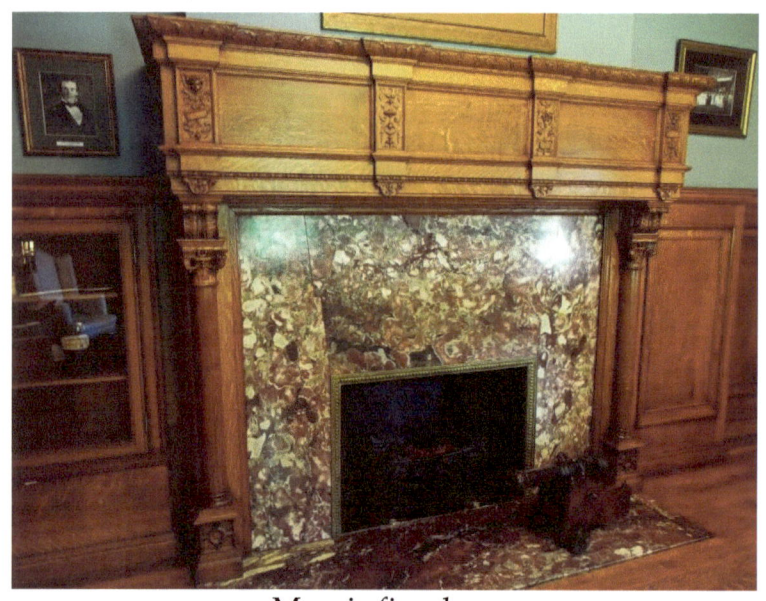

Mosaic fireplace

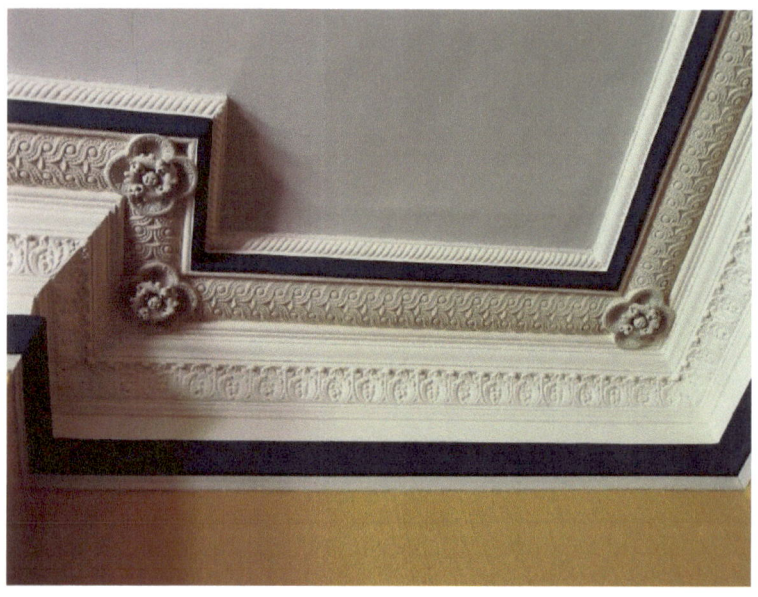

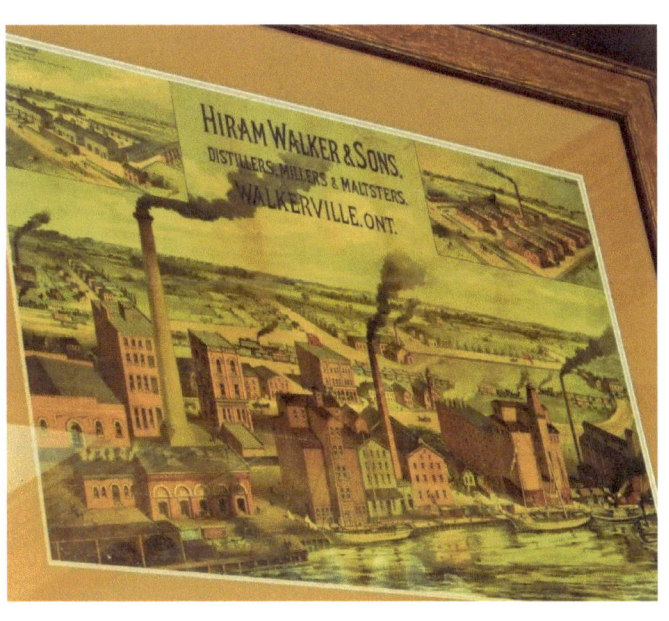

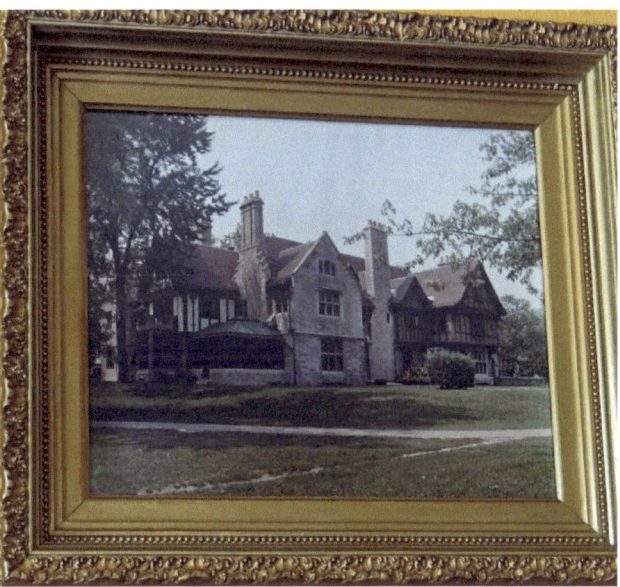

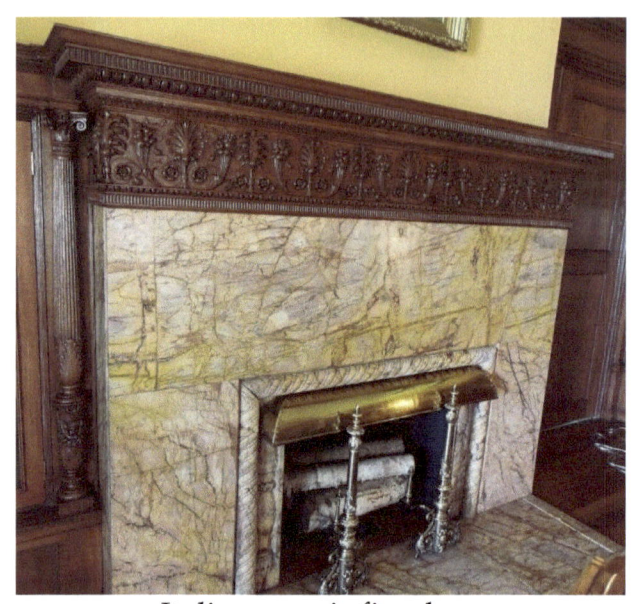

Italian mosaic fireplace

Hiram Walker had an art collection of Canadian artists

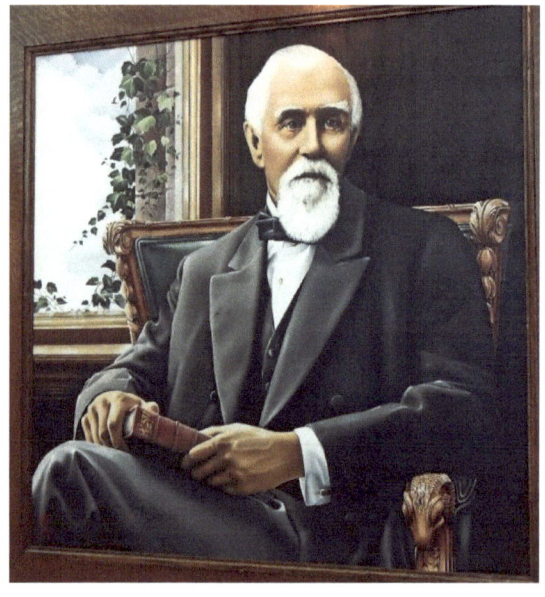

Rum runners were the best customers at this time. The shape and strength of the bottle was changed. It could be strapped to the ankle just above the boot (that is how it got the name bootlegger). Al Capone was a good customer of Edward's. He created a code book for telling about whiskey shipments.

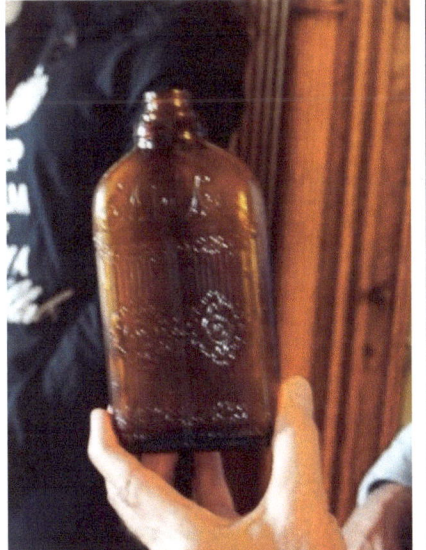 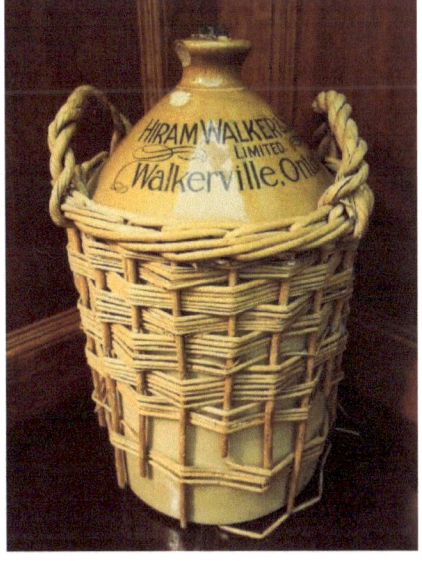

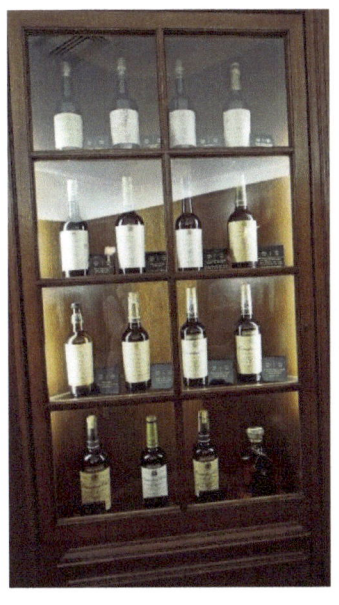 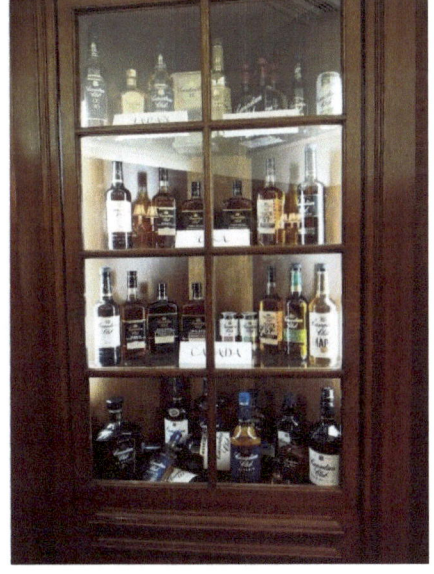

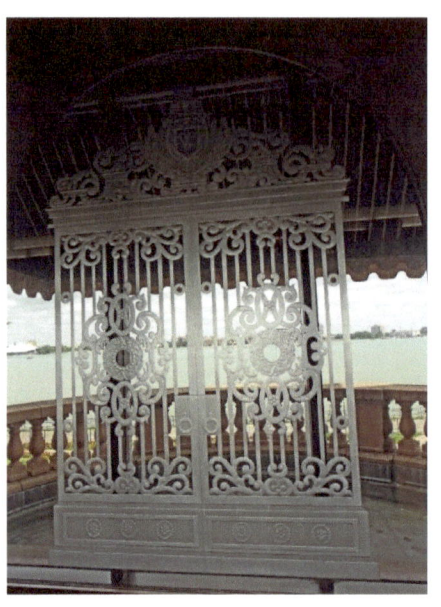

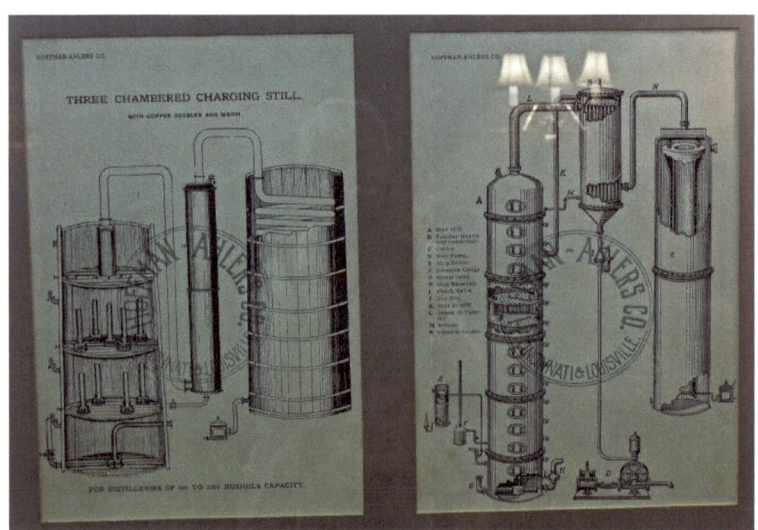

Three-chambered Charging Still

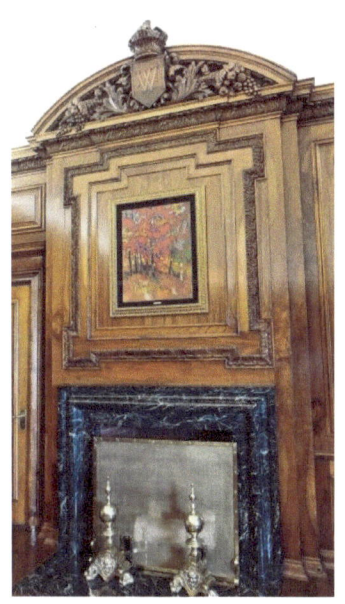
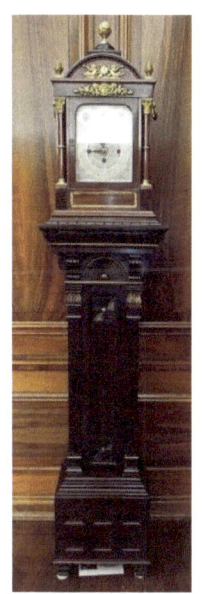
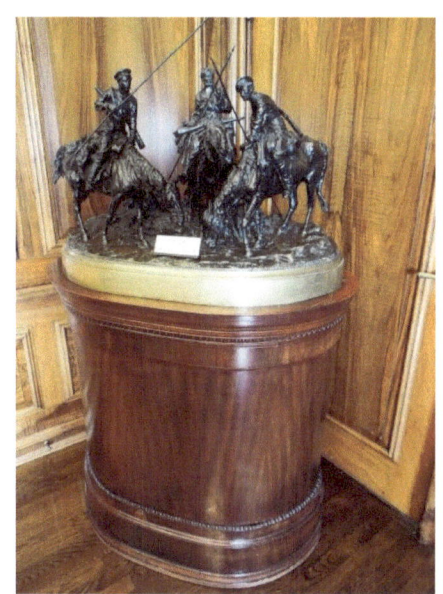

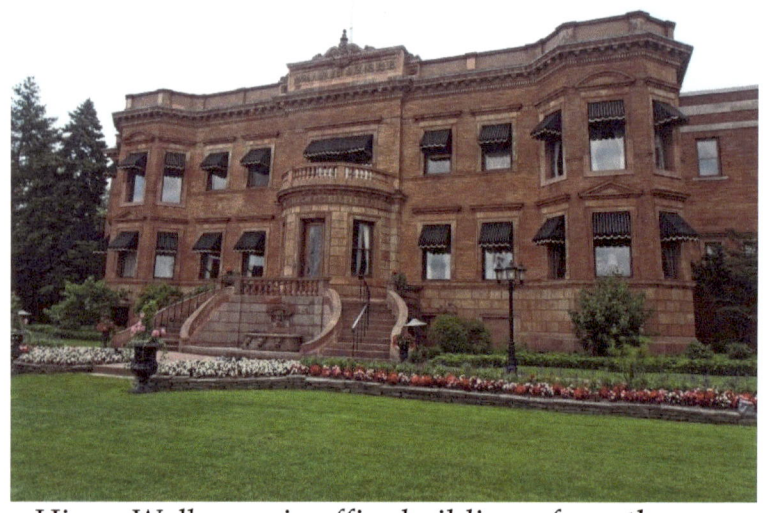

Hiram Walker main office building – from the rear (water side)

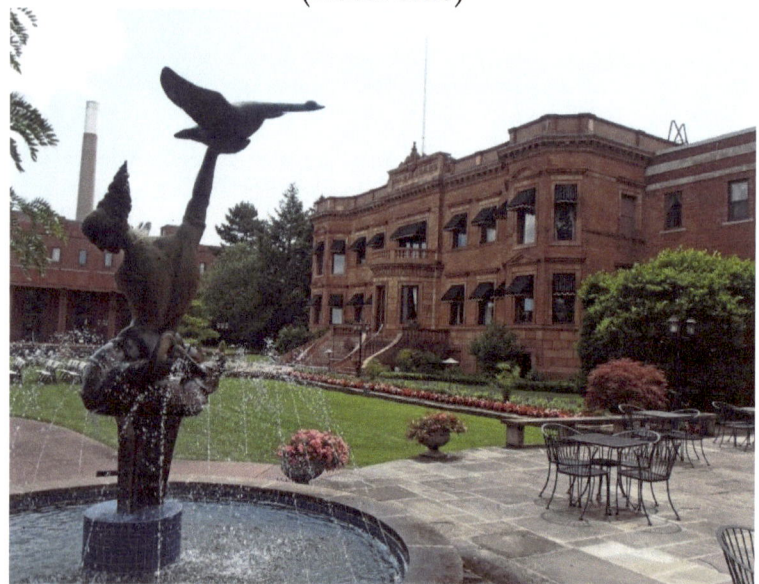

Myth of Creation (fountain) from the Wyandotte and Huron Indian legend portraying the beginning of life by Joseph N. Delauro

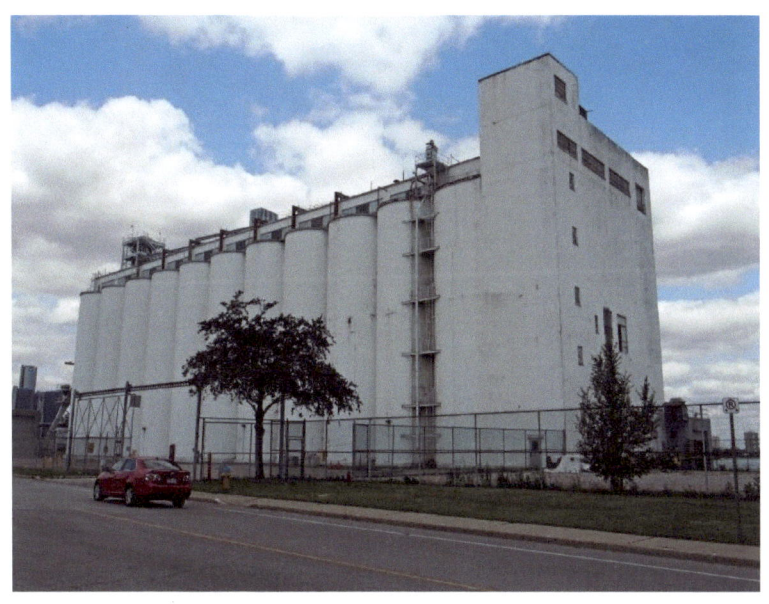

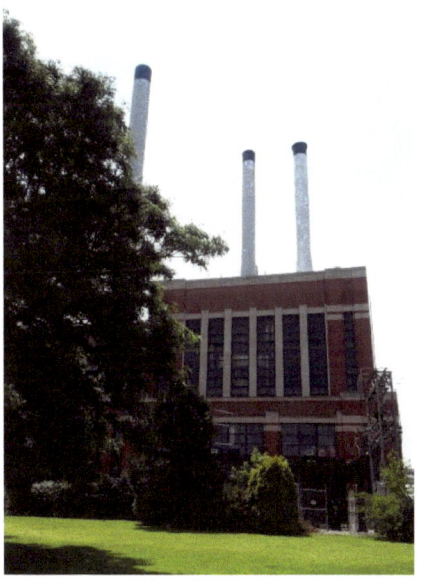

Ford Plant

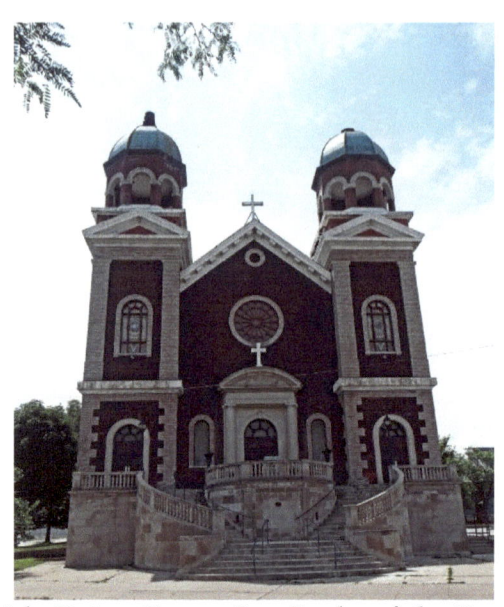

2879 Riverside Drive East – Our Lady of the Rosary Church built 1907-1913 - Romanesque-style brick and stone building could hold about 1,000 people, features two domed bell towers

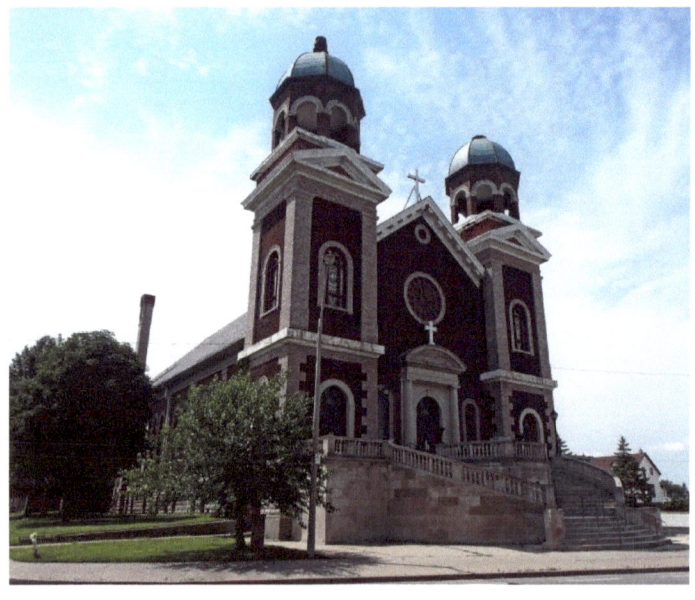

The Blockade

On July 12, 1945 United Auto Workers (UAW) Local 200 went on strike against Ford Motor Company. When word came in November that the Windsor Police Commission requested outside reinforcements from the province, 8,000 workers from other Windsor plants joined the 10,000 strikers. To avoid violent confrontation, protesters created an auto barricade on Sandwich Street East the first block of Drouillard Road. For three days 2000 cars blockaded the entrance to Ford's powerhouse. This event led both sides to agree to binding arbitration which helped end the 99-day strike. When the cars were moved, not one was reported damaged.

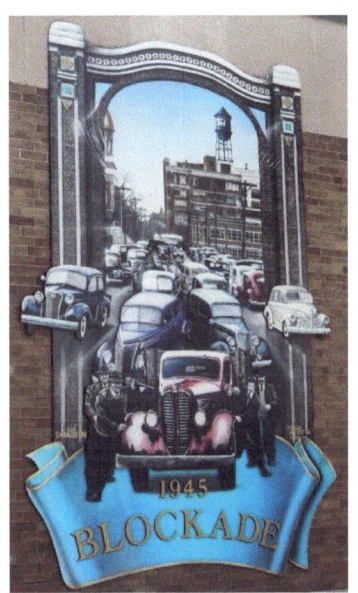

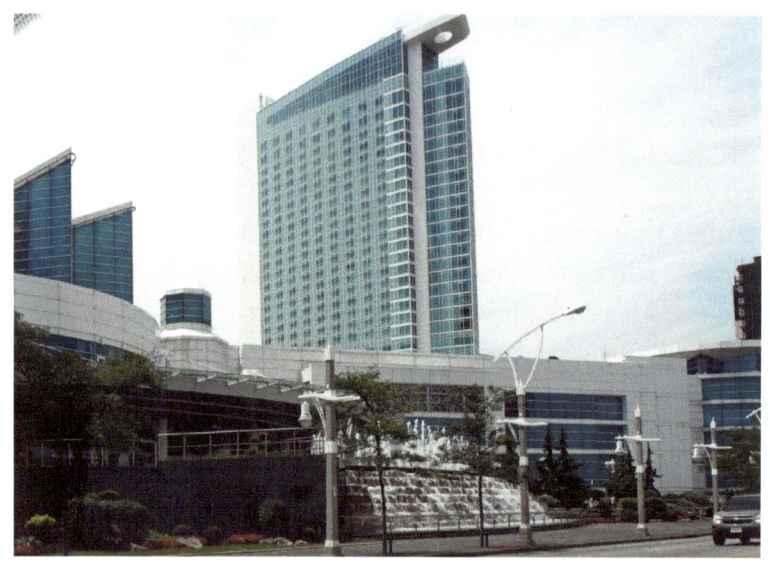

Fountain

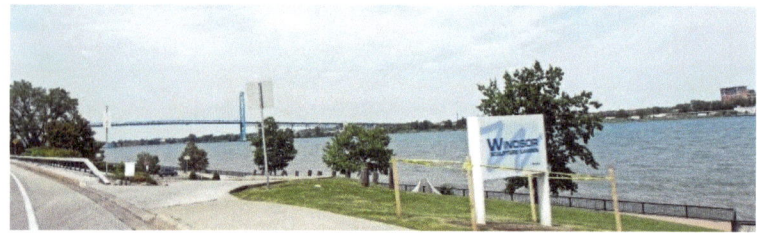

The four-lane Ambassador Bridge is a suspension bridge that connects Detroit, Michigan, U.S.A. with Windsor, Ontario, Canada. It was completed in 1919 with a length of 7,500 feet.

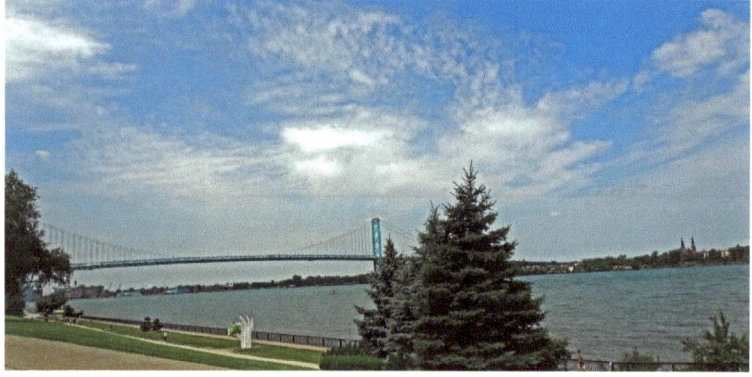

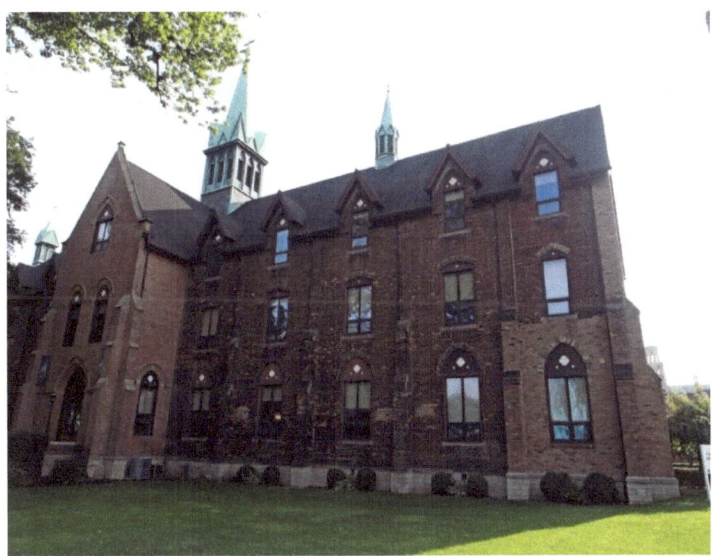

2629 Riverside Drive West - Assumption University has a heritage reaching back to 1857 when it was founded by the Society of Jesus (Jesuit). It is the parent of the University of Windsor and is administered by the Congregation of St. Basil, the Basilian Fathers. When the University of Windsor was established in 1963, Assumption University entered into federation with it and became the Catholic university within the University of Windsor.

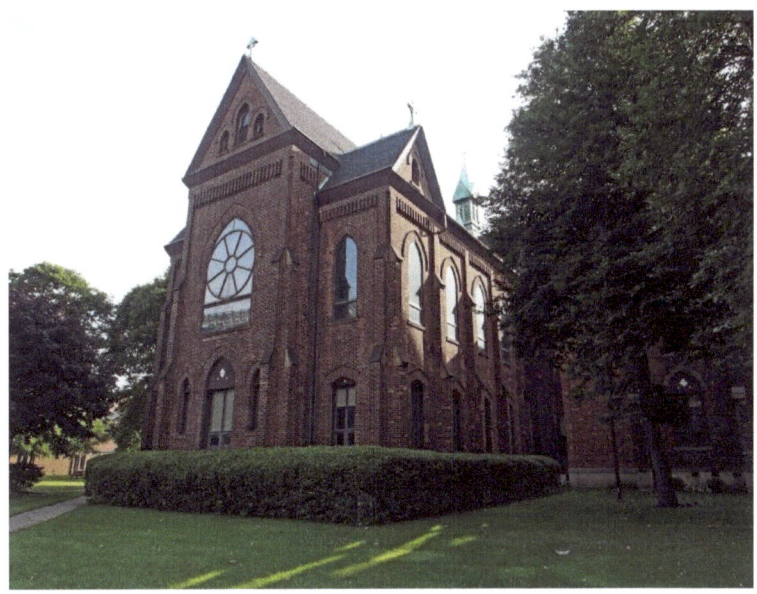

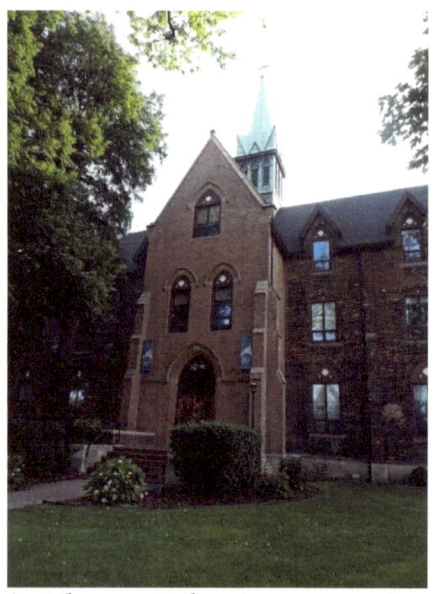

Assumption is a privately operated, autonomous university separate from the University of Windsor and yet an integral part of it. It has retained its degree-granting powers and graduates students within the area of theology, as well as granting honorary degrees.

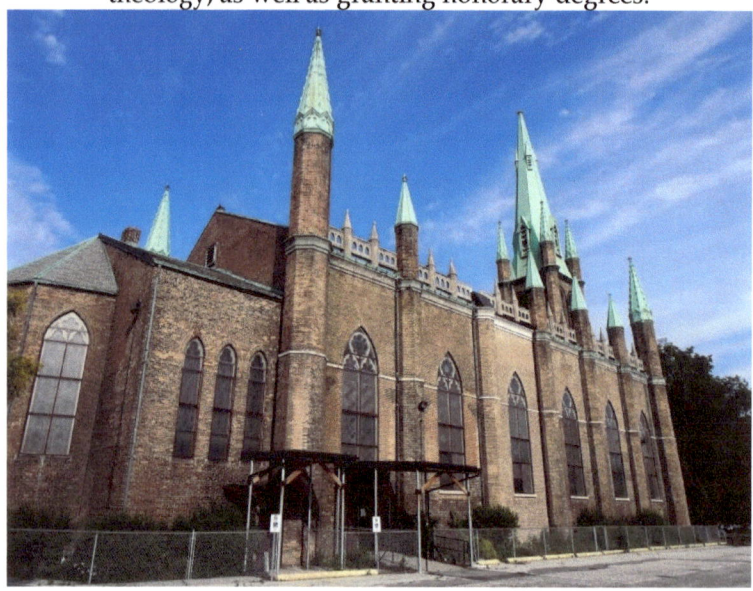

Buttresses with finials, lancet windows

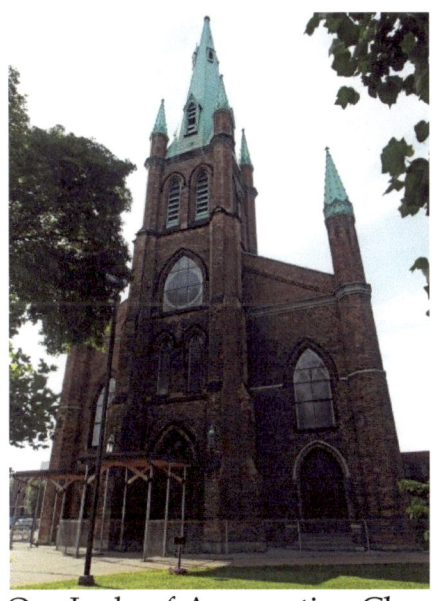
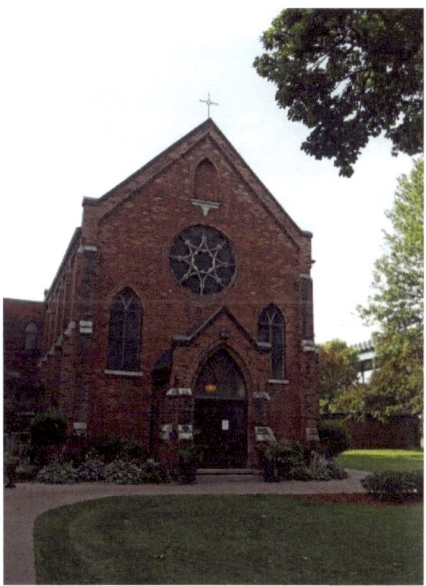

Our Lady of Assumption Church   Rosary Chapel
1845   rose window, lancet windows
Buttresses, finials

Sandwich Village

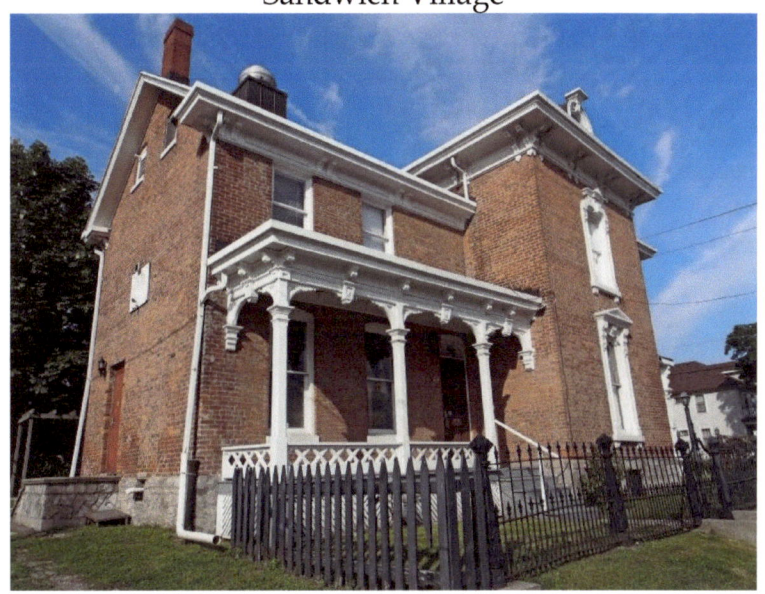

3203 Peter Street - Mason-Girardot House - 1877

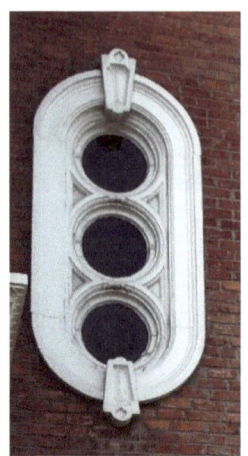

"Traffic light" window

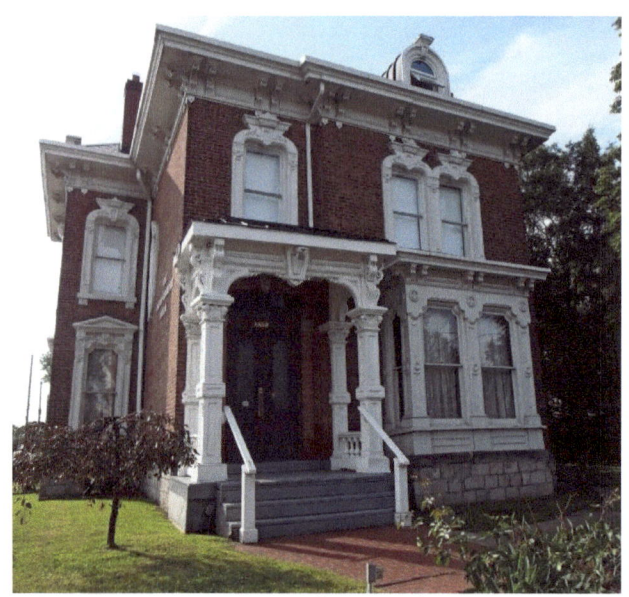

3203 Peter Street – Victorian Italianate/Second Empire – detailed façade, carved entryway supported by square, decorative columns; keystone motif above windows and above hooded window on third floor; cornice is boxed with frieze and brackets

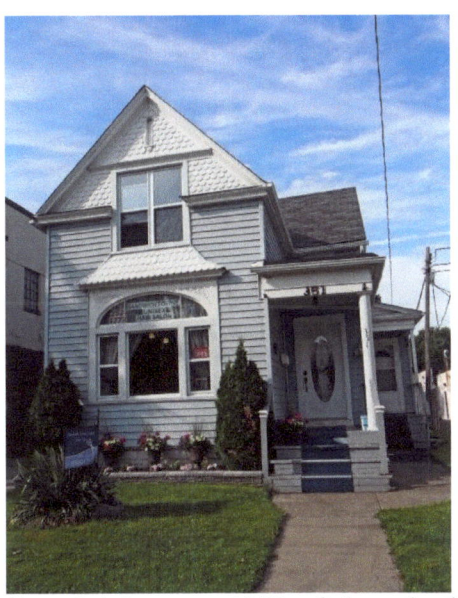

351 Mill Street - Langlois house – 1888 – fish scale shingles on gable

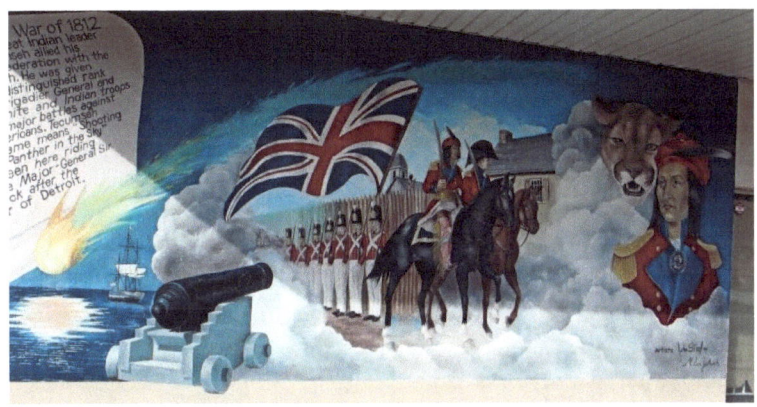

Mill Street Mural

In the War of 1812, the great Indian leader Tecumseh allied his Confederation with the British. He was given the distinguished rank of Brigadier-General and led white and Indian troops in four major battles against the Americans. Tecumseh whose name means "Shooting Star" or "Panther in the Sky" can be seen here riding along beside Major-General Sir Isaac Brock after the surrender of Detroit.

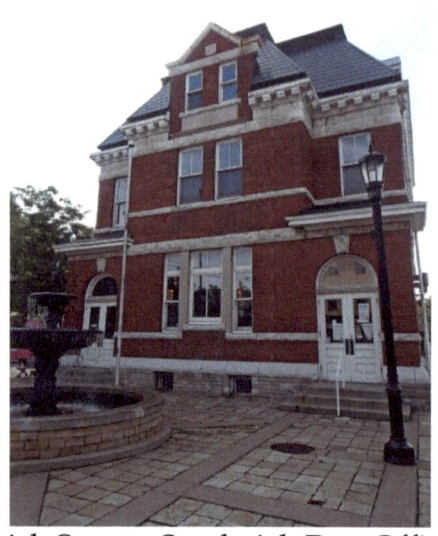

3201 Sandwich Street - Sandwich Post Office built 1905
Voussoirs with keystones over rounded doors;
dentilled cornice

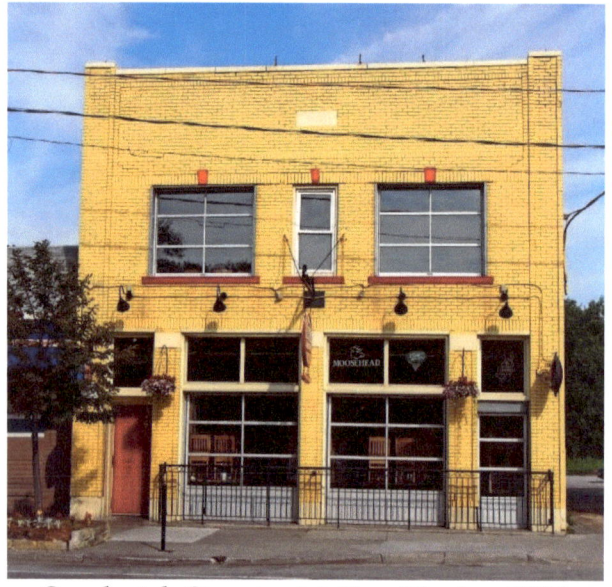

Sandwich Street – McKee Block – 1921

Mural on side of Medical Building

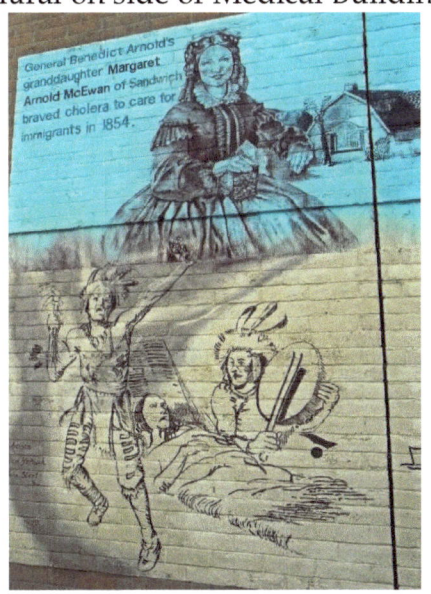

General Benedict Arnold's granddaughter Margaret Arnold McEwan of Sandwich braved cholera to care for immigrants in 1854.

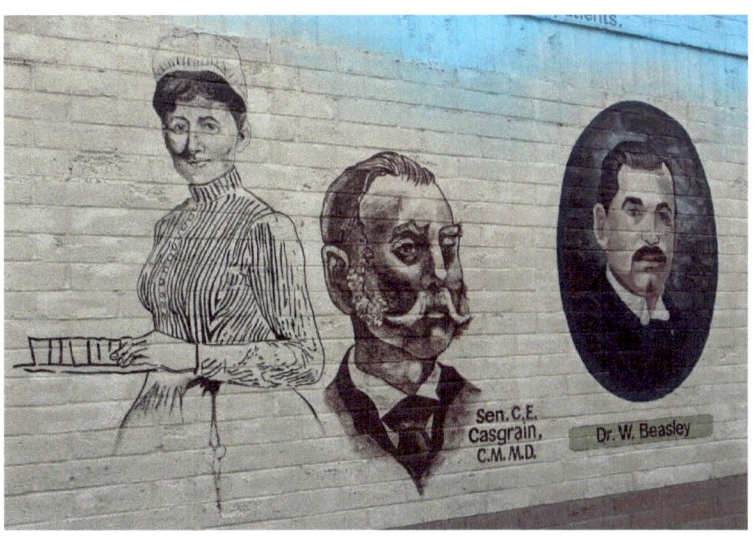

Senator C.E. Casgrain MD, Dr. W. Beasley

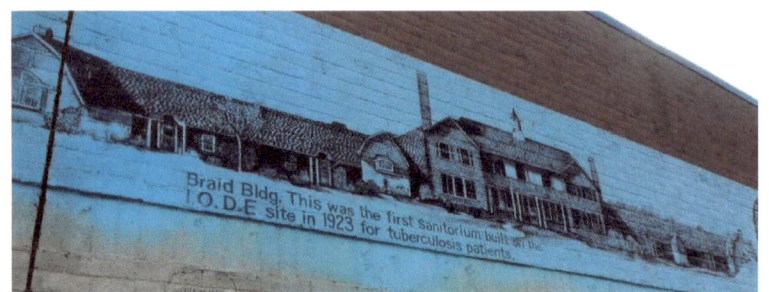

Braid Building – the was the first sanatorium built on the I.O.D.E. site for tuberculosis patients

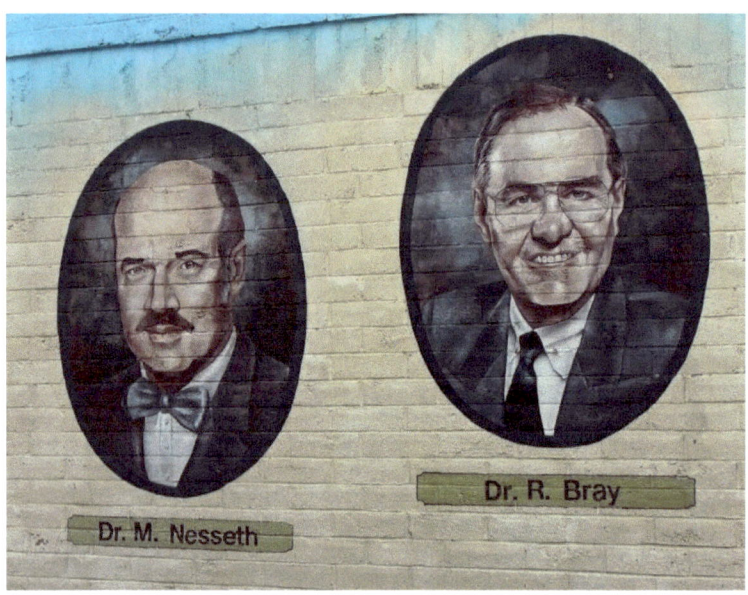

Doctors M. Nesseth and R. Bray

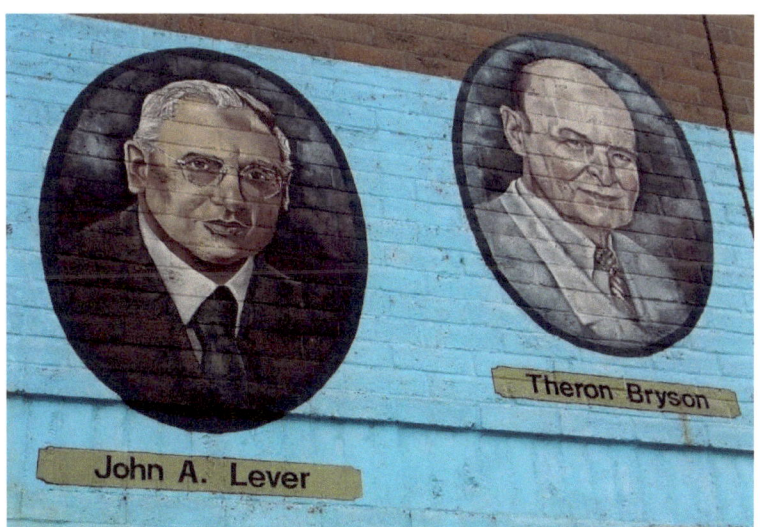

John A. Lever and Theron Bryson

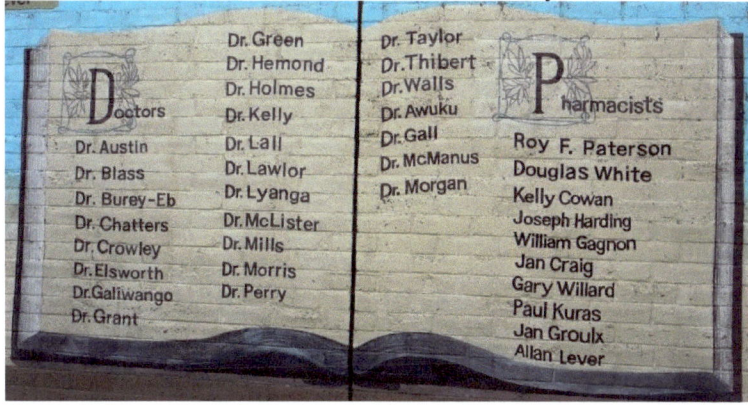

Doctors

Dr. Austin
Dr. Blass
Dr. Burey-Eb
Dr. Chatters
Dr. Crowley
Dr. Elsworth
Dr. Galiwango
Dr. Grant

Dr. Green
Dr. Hemond
Dr. Holmes
Dr. Kelly
Dr. Lall
Dr. Lawlor
Dr. Lyanga
Dr. McLister
Dr. Mills
Dr. Morris
Dr. Perry

Dr. Taylor
Dr. Thibert
Dr. Walls
Dr. Awuku
Dr. Gall
Dr. McManus
Dr. Morgan

Pharmacists

Roy F. Paterson
Douglas White
Kelly Cowan
Joseph Harding
William Gagnon
Jan Craig
Gary Willard
Paul Kuras
Jan Groulx
Allan Lever

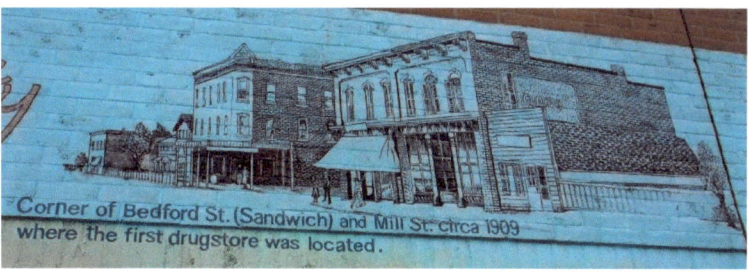

Corner of Bedford Street (Sandwich) and Mill Street c. 1909
where the first drugstore was located

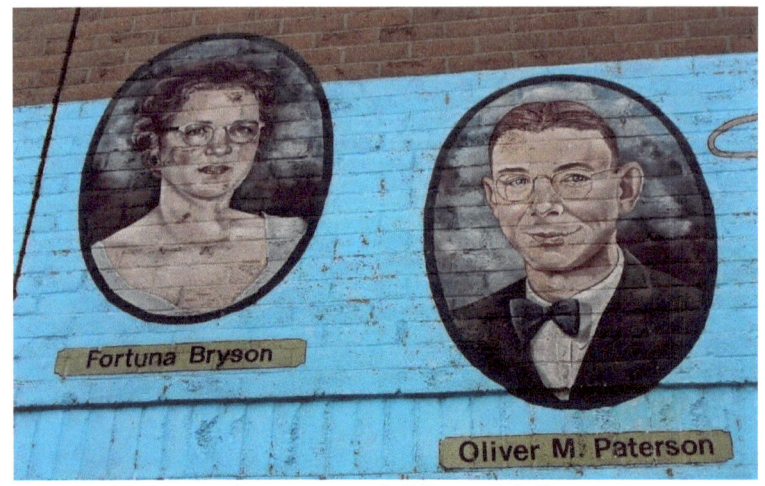

Fortuna Bryson and Oliver M. Paterson

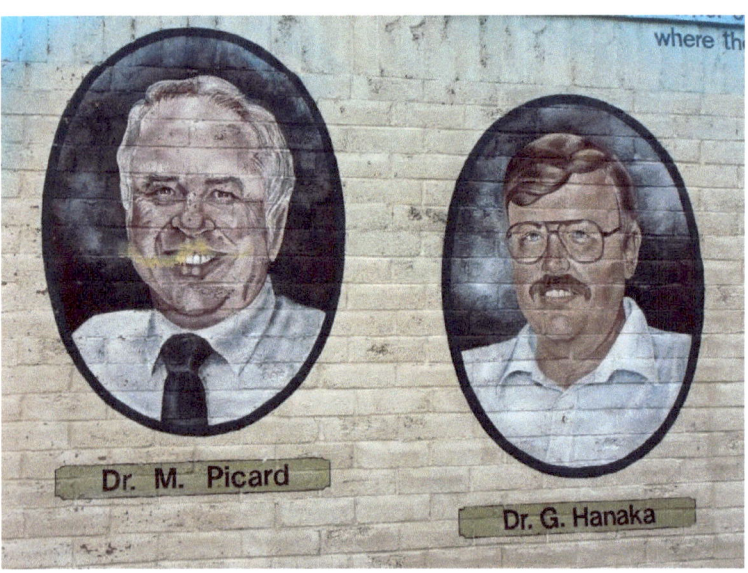

Doctors M. Picard and G. Hanaka

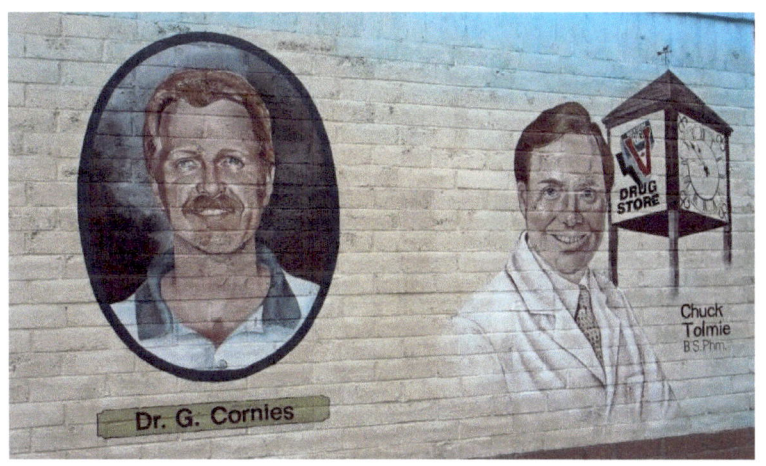

Dr. G. Cornies and Chuck Tolmie

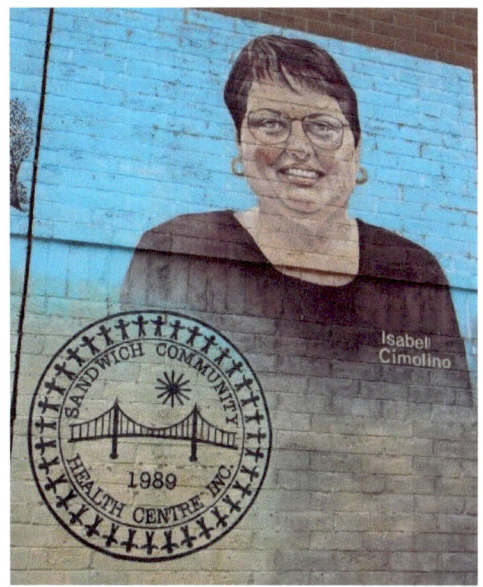

Isabel Cimolino

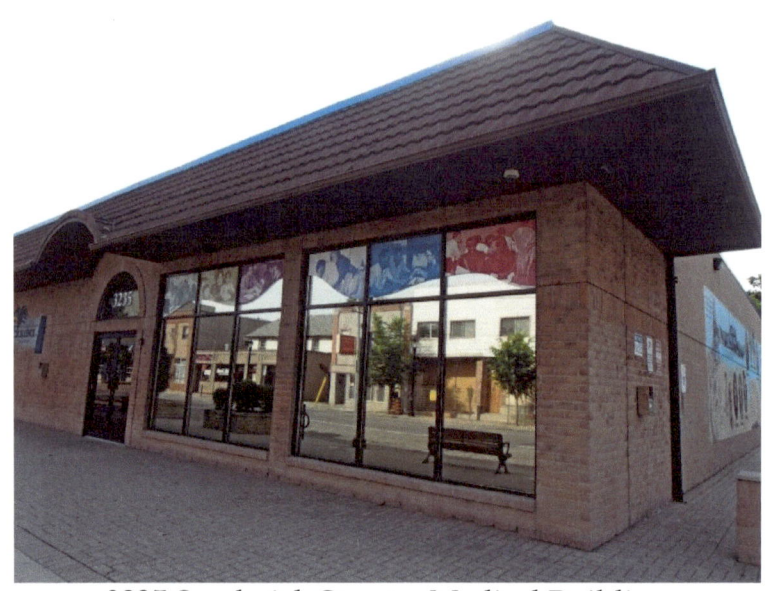

3235 Sandwich Street – Medical Building

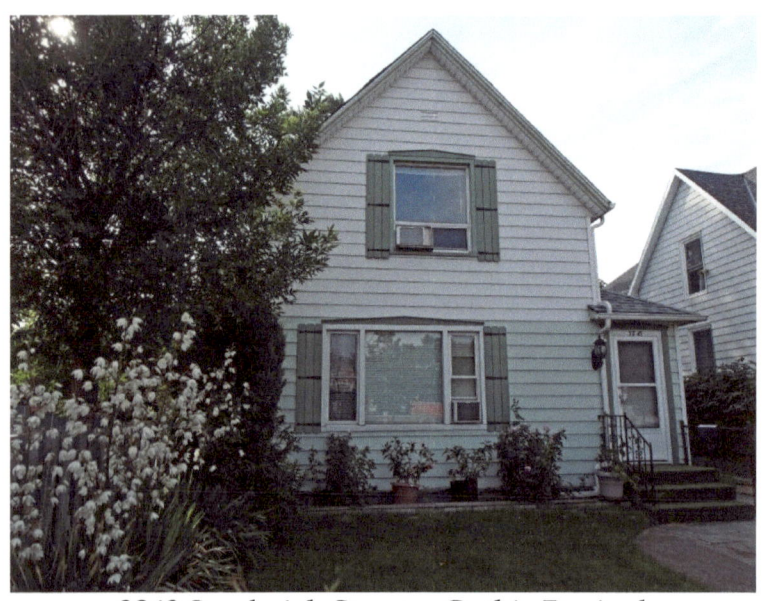

3243 Sandwich Street – Gothic Revival

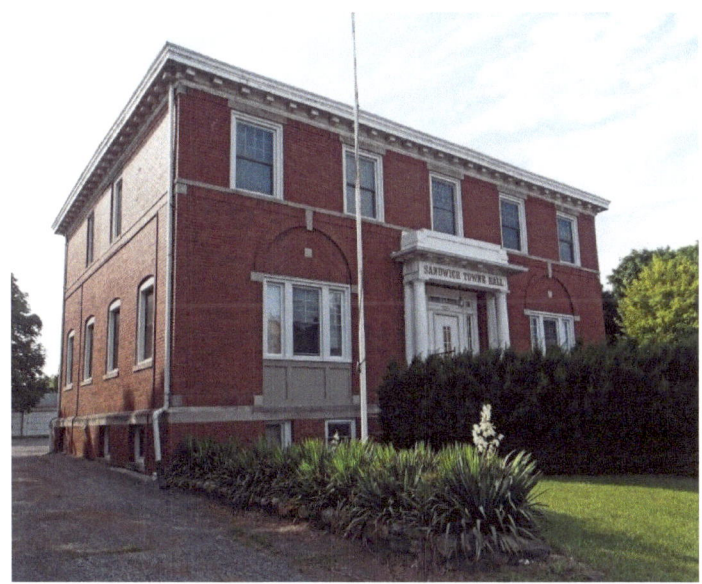

3255 Sandwich Street – Town Hall – low pitched roof, symmetry, blind brick arcades suggest the Georgian style; portico with columned entryway and main door with sidelights and transom; above the first floor tripartite windows is a blind arcade of bricks laid in a chevron pattern. A dentilled cornice encircles the building as does the continuous sill under the first and second floor windows.

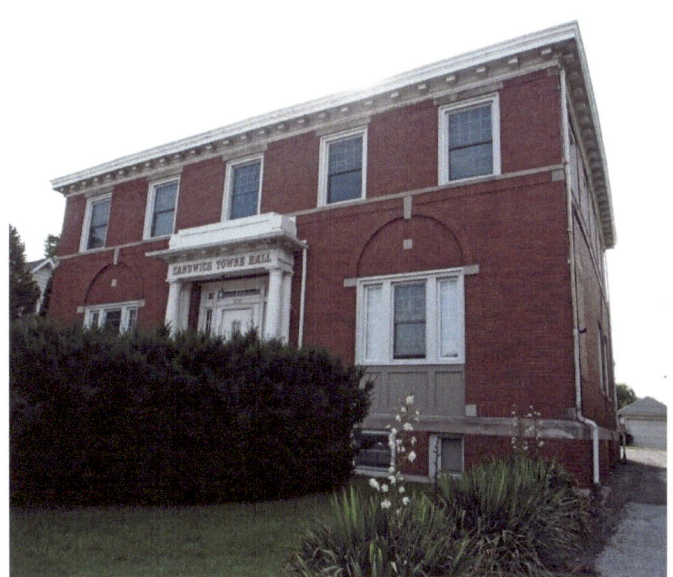

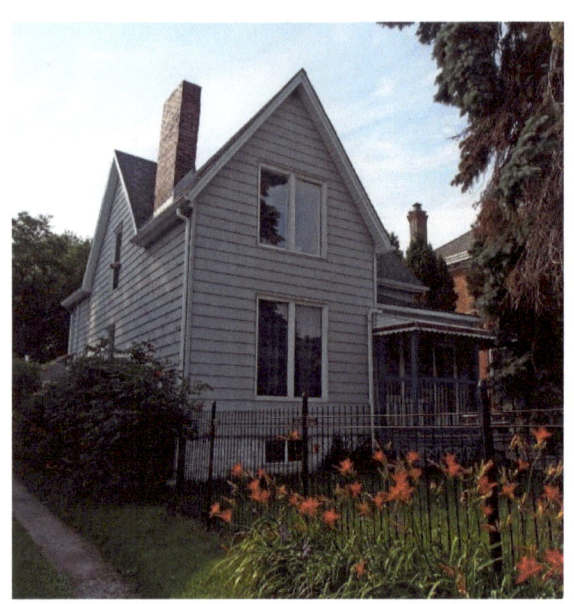

3249 Sandwich Street - Gothic

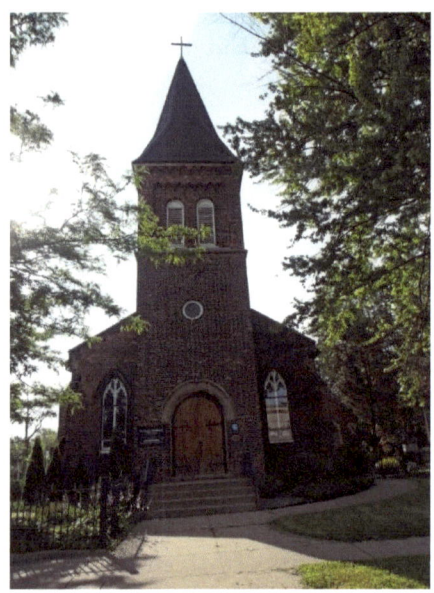

St. John's Anglican Church – 1852-1871 – Gothic style with
Norman tower

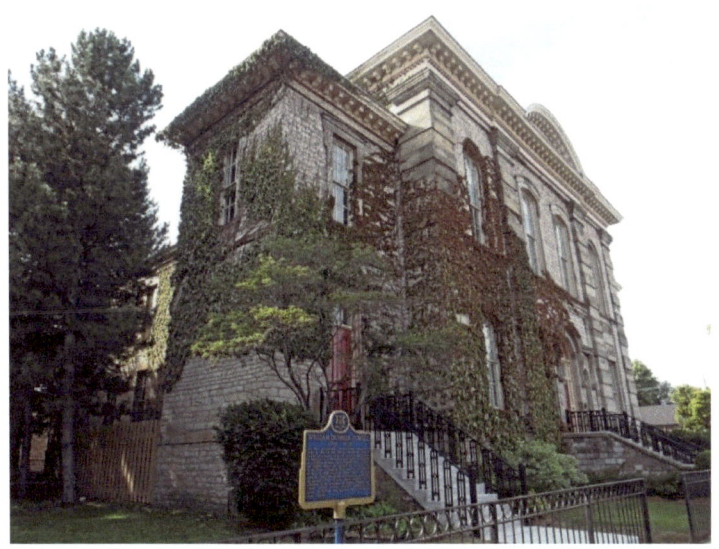

3277 Sandwich Street – Mackenzie Hall – District Court House and Gaol - when–the British withdrew from Detroit in 1796 they transferred the courts of the Western District to Sandwich (Windsor) – this building constructed in 1856 in Renaissance Revival style; a facade broken with pilasters which give strong vertical lines; the main entrance has side lights and a fanlight; it is constructed of Anderdon limestone and Ohio sandstone. The carving above the main doorway represents the seal of the Western District of Upper Canada.

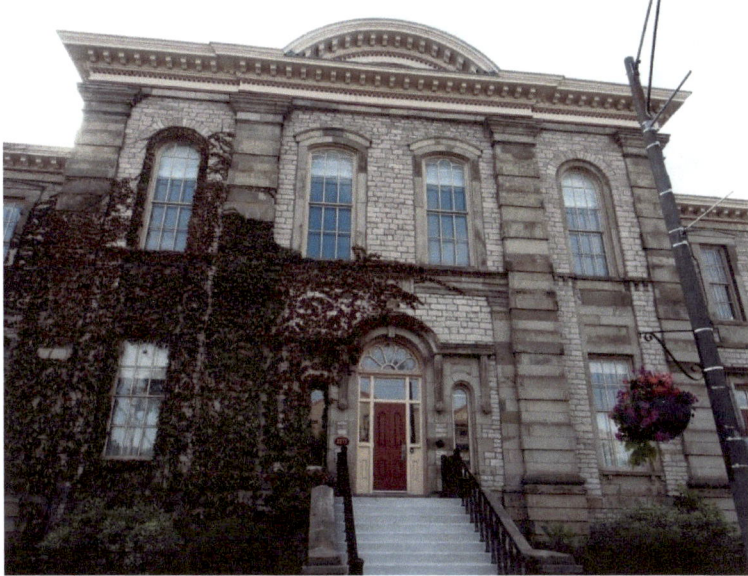

Following the cession of Detroit to the United States in 1794, and the withdrawal of the British garrison two years later, many residents moved to the Canadian side of the river where they founded the community of Sandwich.

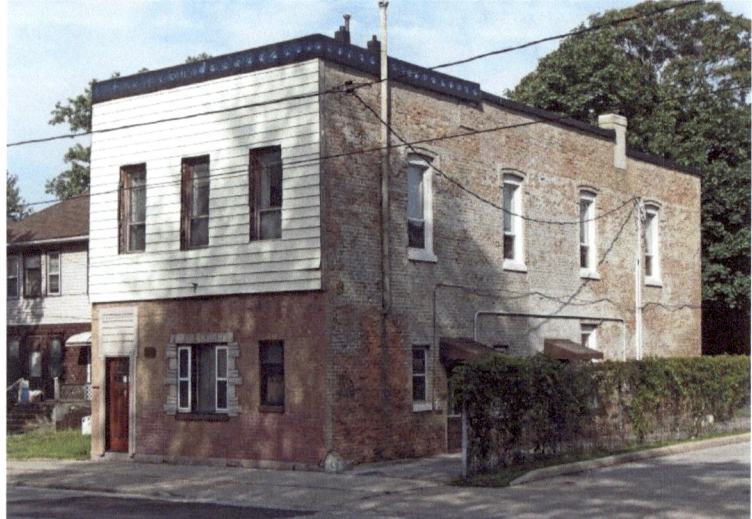

3330 Sandwich Street c. 1890 – two storey brick building

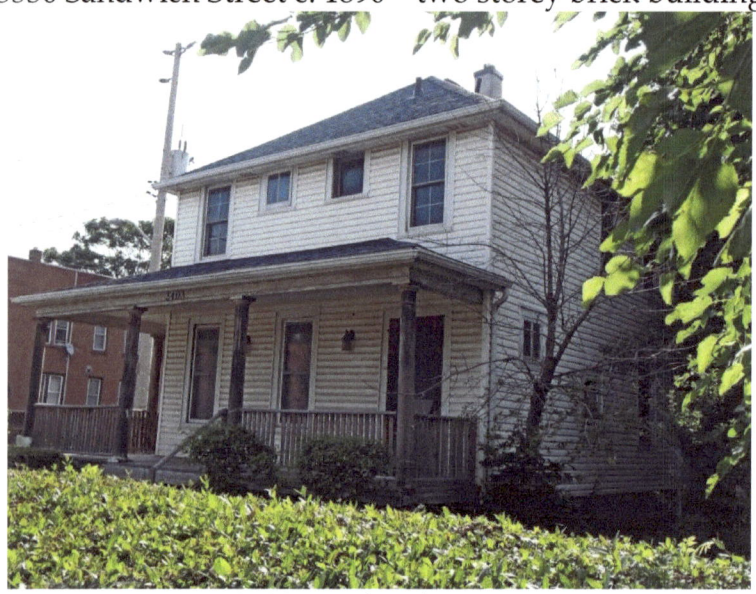

3403 Sandwich Street

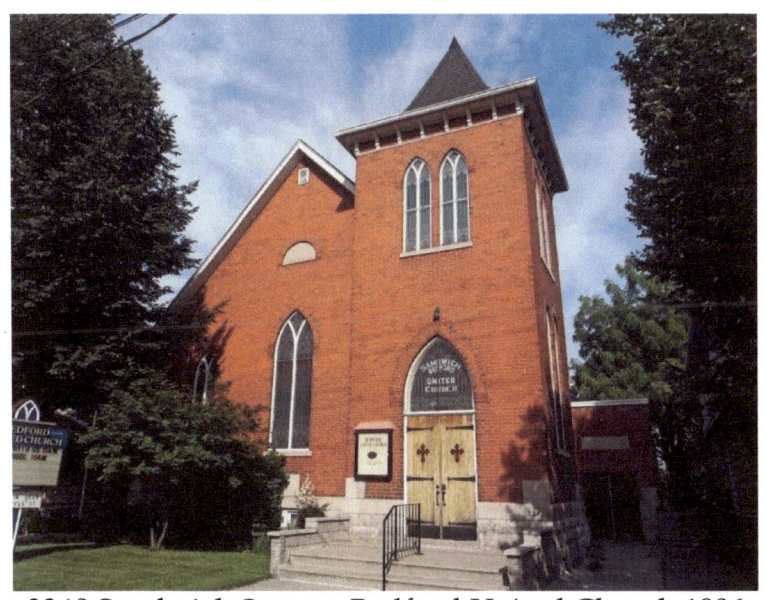

3340 Sandwich Street – Bedford United Church 1906
Gothic Revival style with Romanesque tower – red brick with
rusticated masonry

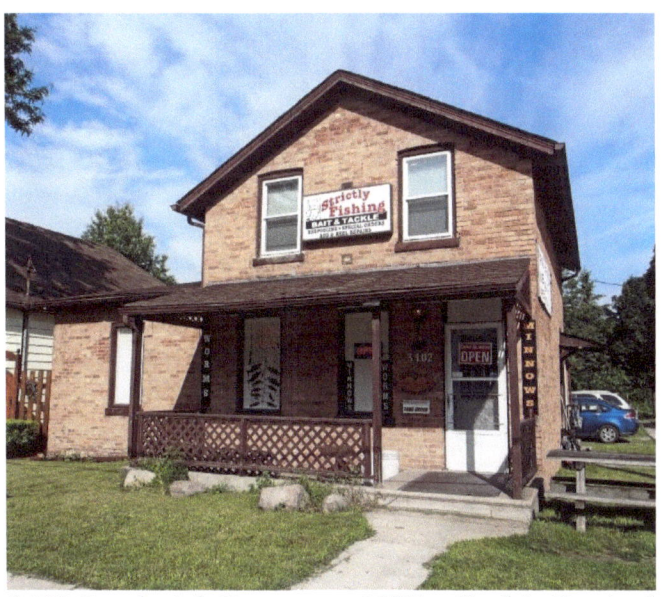

3402 Sandwich Street – c. 1855 – Gothic Revival

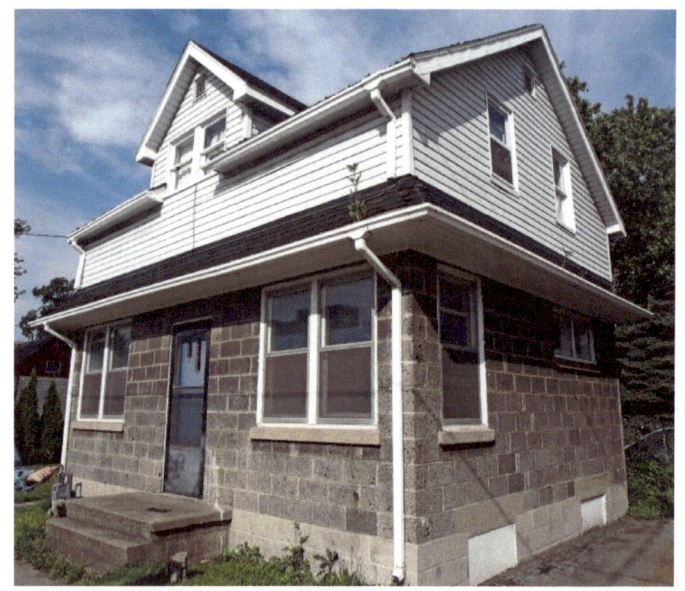

Sandwich Street - vernacular

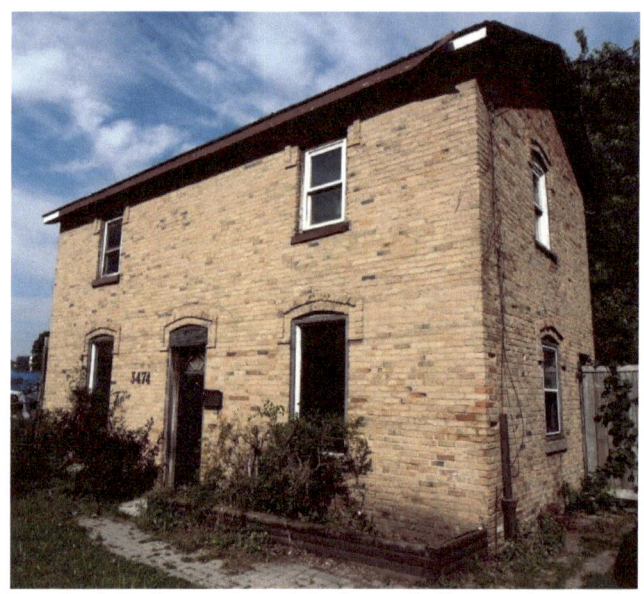

3474 Sandwich Street – gabled roof, flat-arched windows

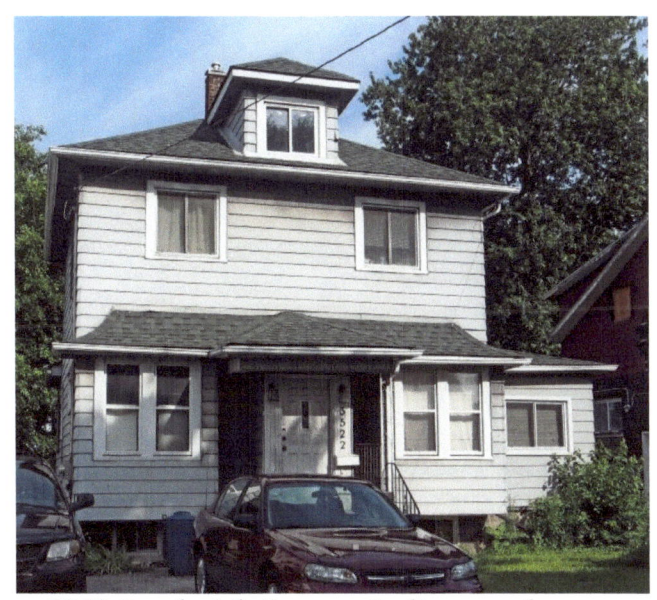

3522 Sandwich Street – Italianate, dormer

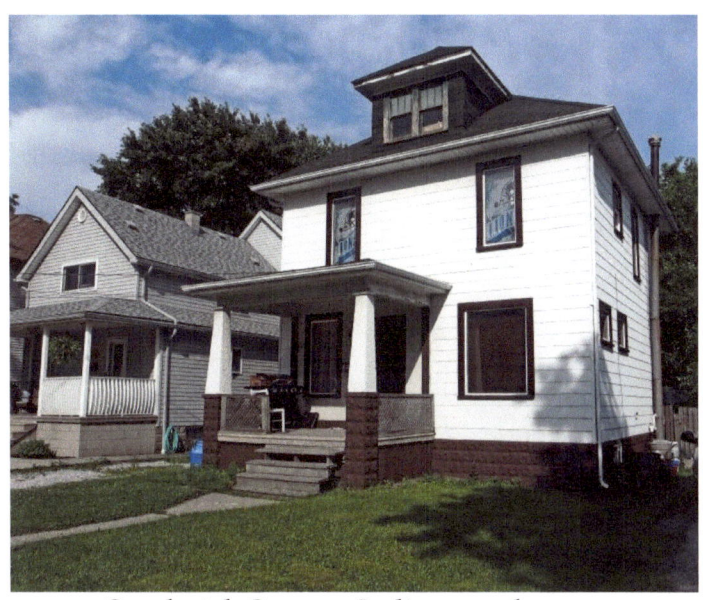

Sandwich Street – Italianate, dormer

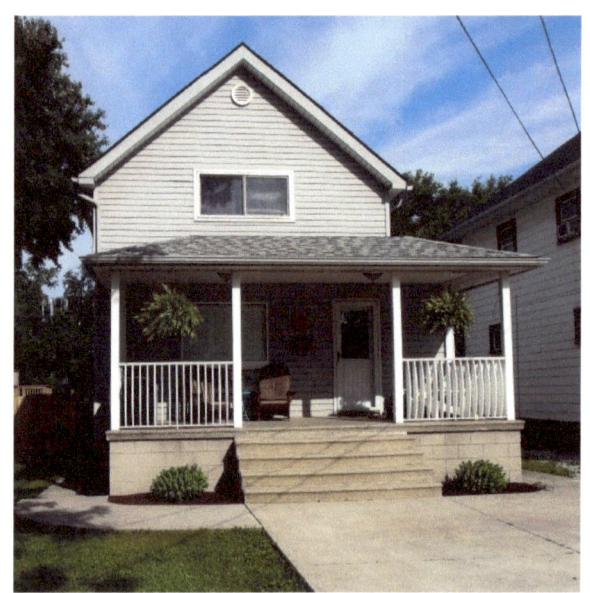

3530 Sandwich Street – Gothic Revival

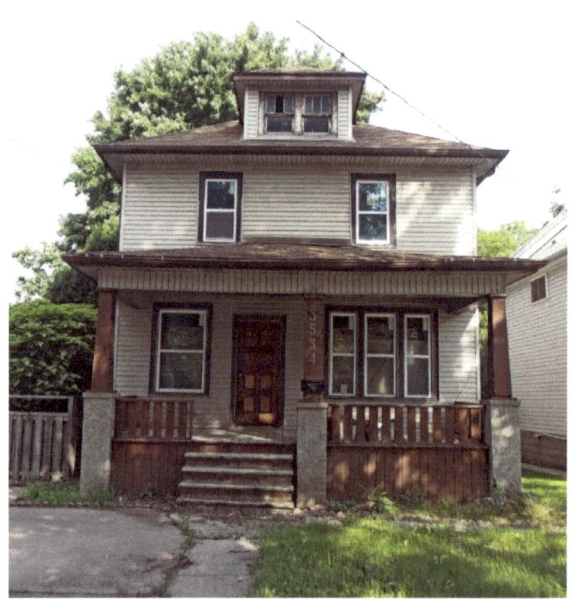

3534 Sandwich Street – Italianate, dormer

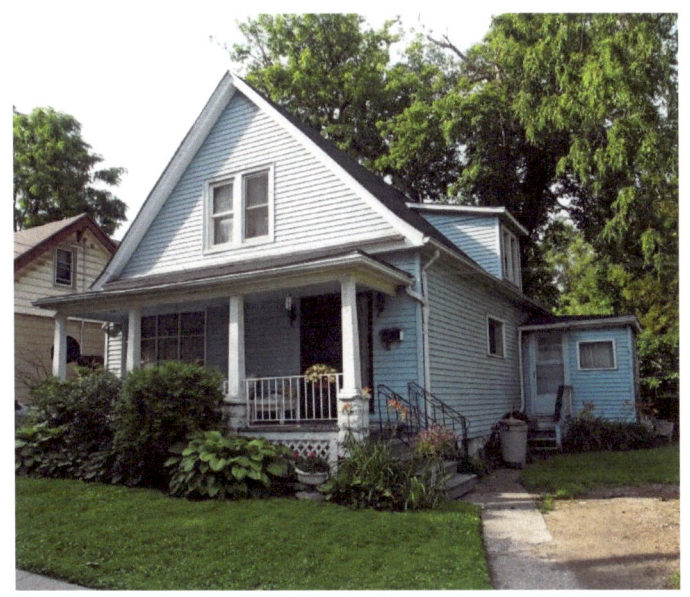

375 Peter Street

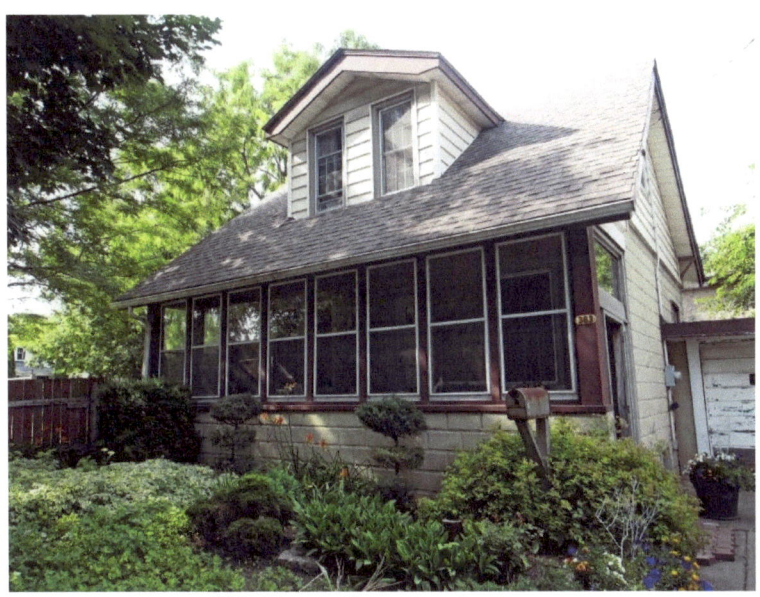

383 Peter Street - dormer

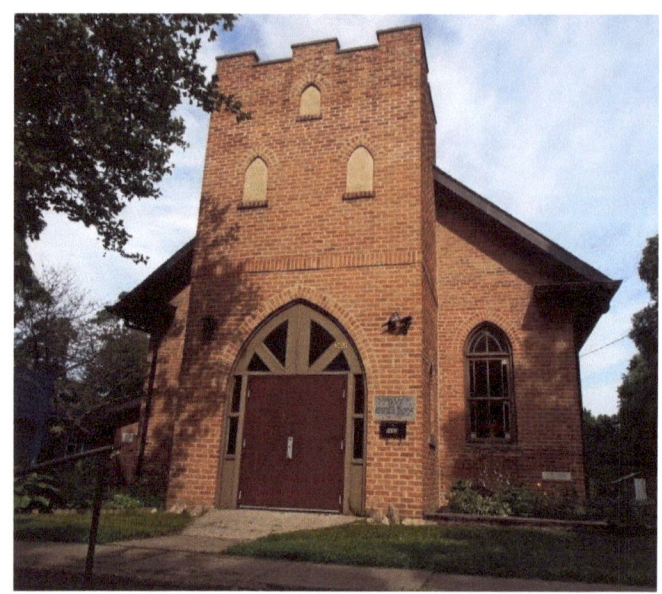

3652 Peter Street - Sandwich First Baptist Church erected in 1851 on land donated by the Crown to serve the rapidly increasing numbers of Black Underground Railroad settlers. This church received, sheltered and assisted many of these new arrivals.

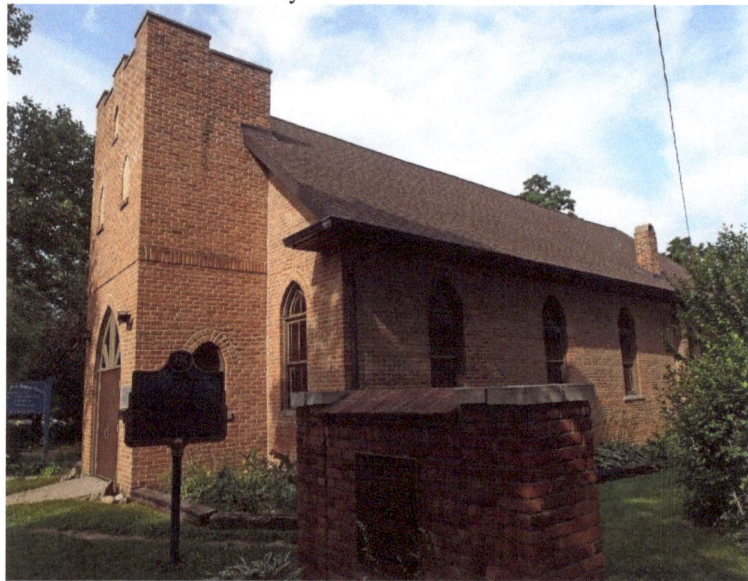

The church was hand-made with Detroit River clay by escaping slaves and free Blacks as payment for a meal and safe haven.

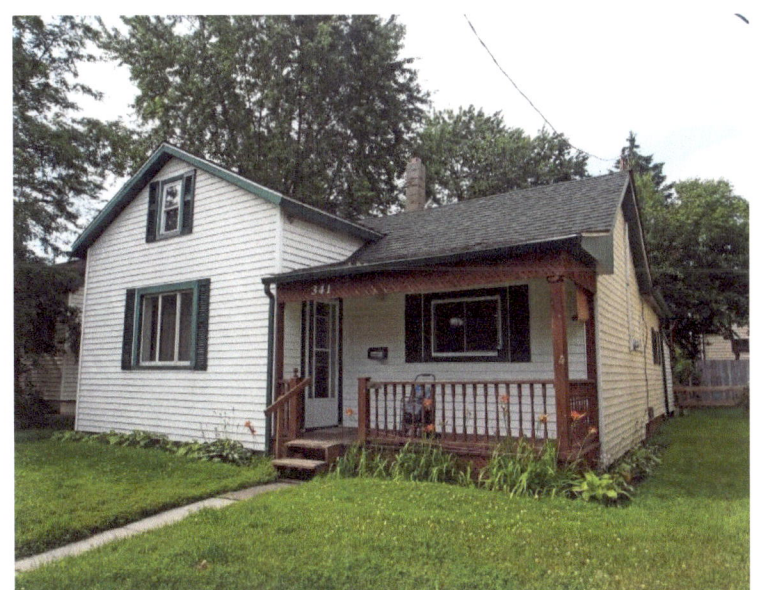

341 Peter Street

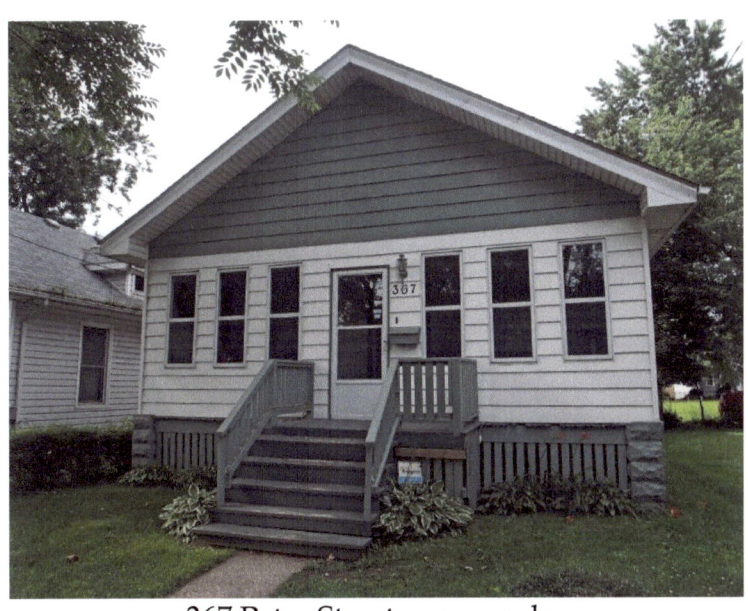

367 Peter Street - vernacular

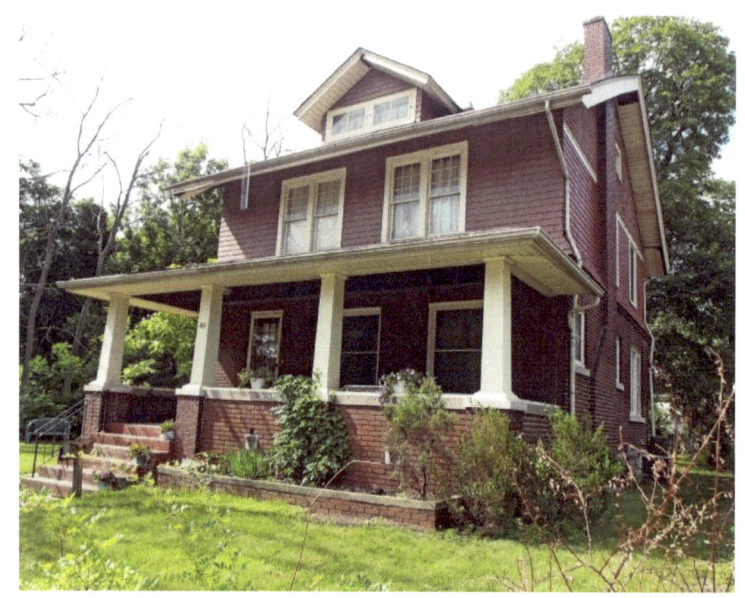

411 Prince Street – vernacular, dormer

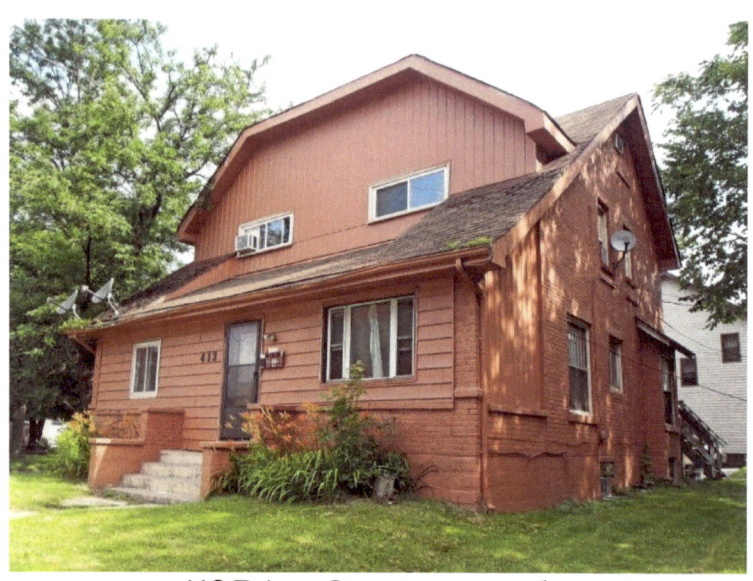

412 Prince Street - vernacular

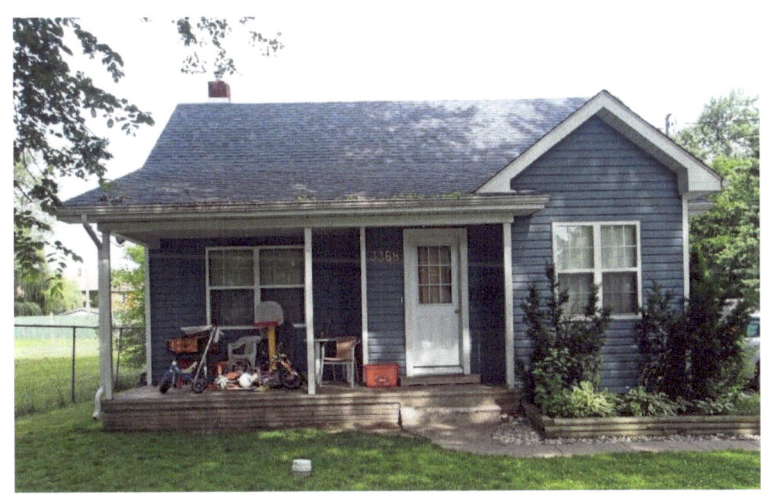

3368 Peter Street

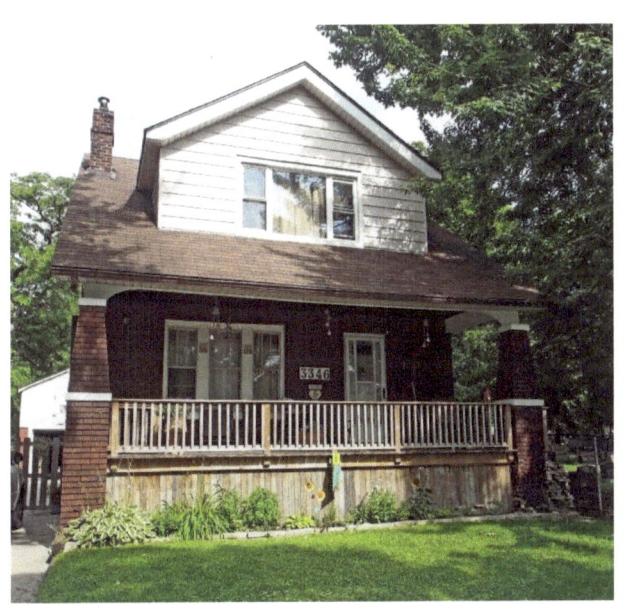

3346 Peter Street

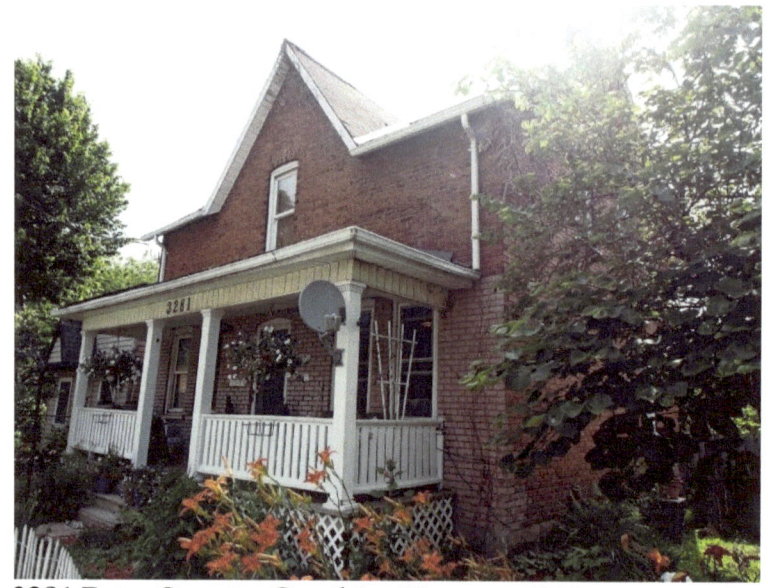

3281 Peter Street – Gauthier House – 1911 – vernacular "Ontario House" – lateral-gabled roof and steeply pitched gable on the street front

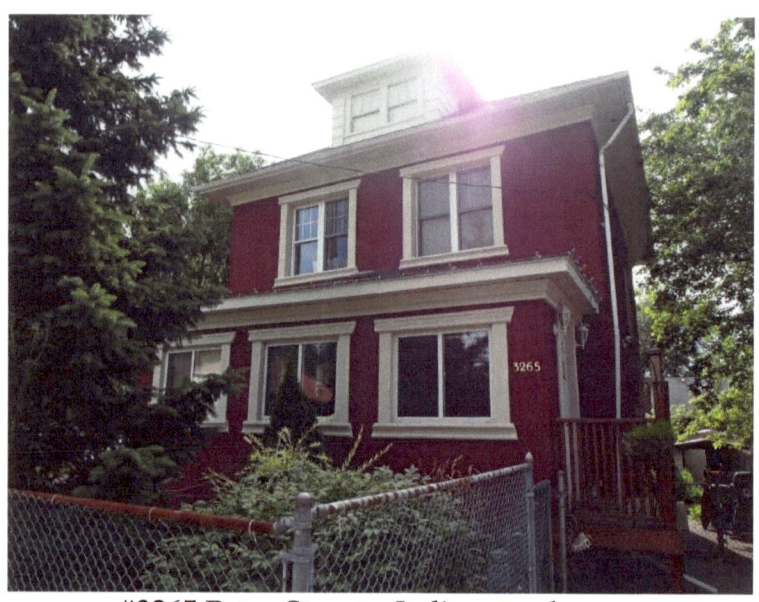

#3265 Peter Street – Italianate, dormer

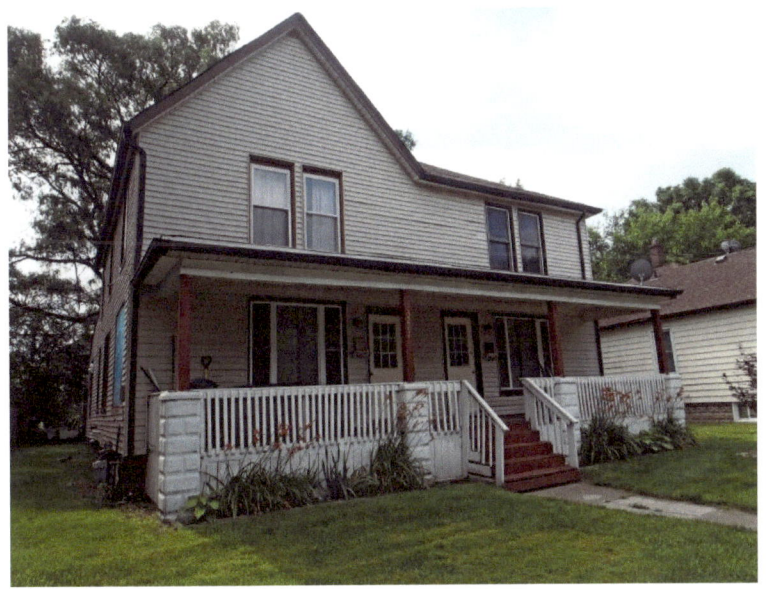

3227 Peter Street - vernacular

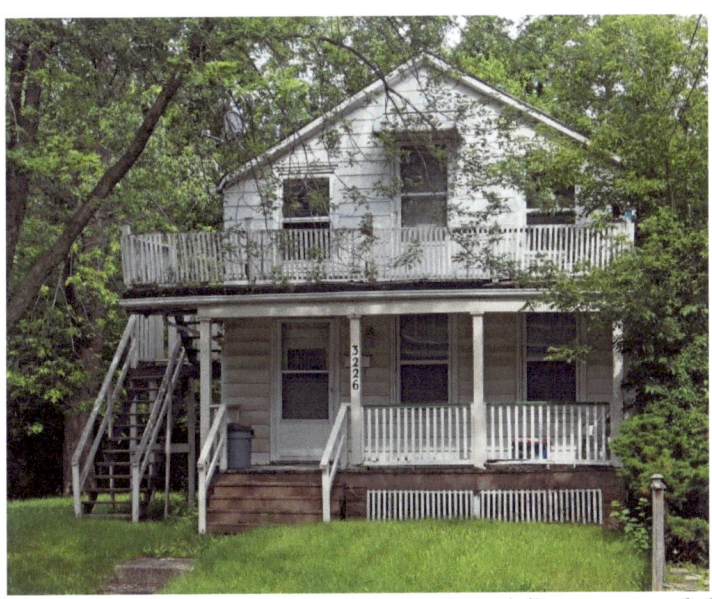

3226 Peter Street – Gothic Revival, 2nd floor verandah

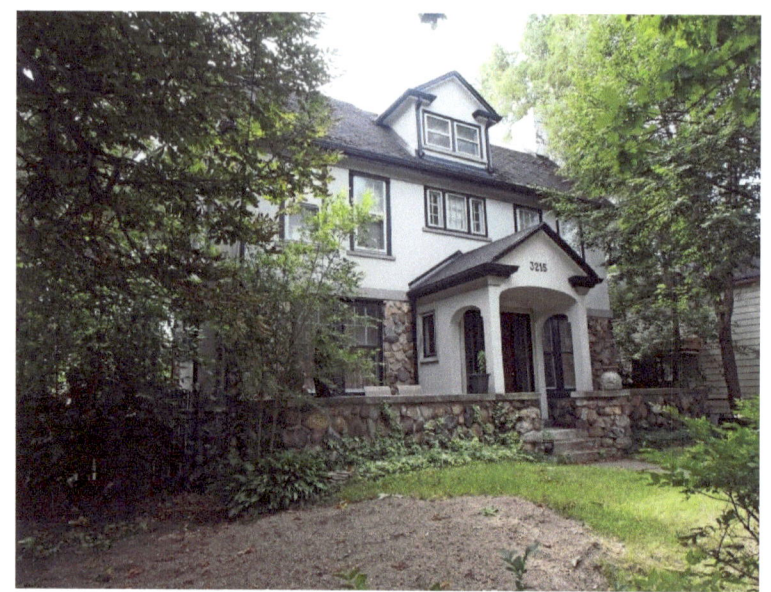

3215 Peter Street, dormer, entrance

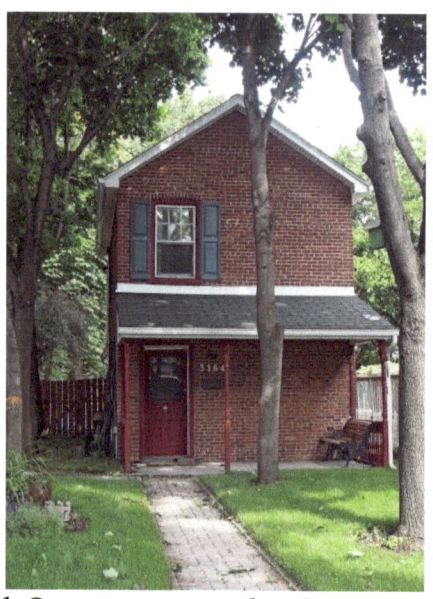

3164 Sandwich Street – vernacular Georgian cottage - 1890

The Founding of Sandwich

In 1701 the French built a military and trading post at Detroit that governed this area of Canada. Jesuit Father Richard de La Richardie came in 1728 at the request of the Huron Indians to establish "The Mission of the Assumption of the Blessed Virgin Mary among the Hurons". The Huron Mission moved away from the liquor bartered by merchants and fur traders at Detroit to the south shore near present day Sandwich and built the first Assumption Church as seen here.

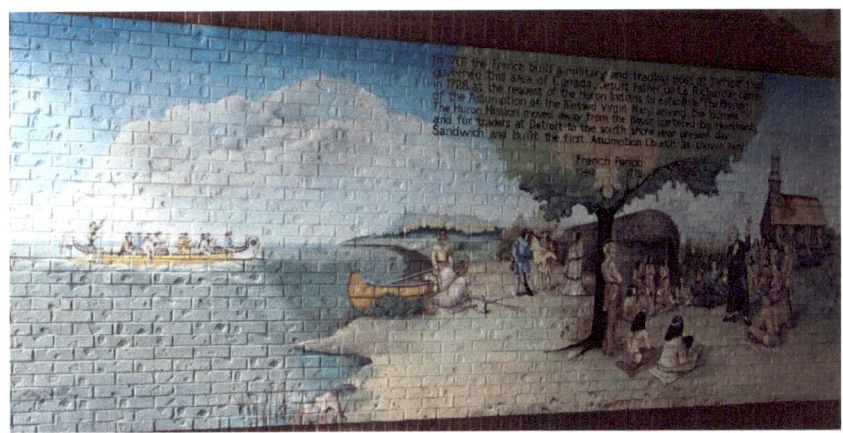

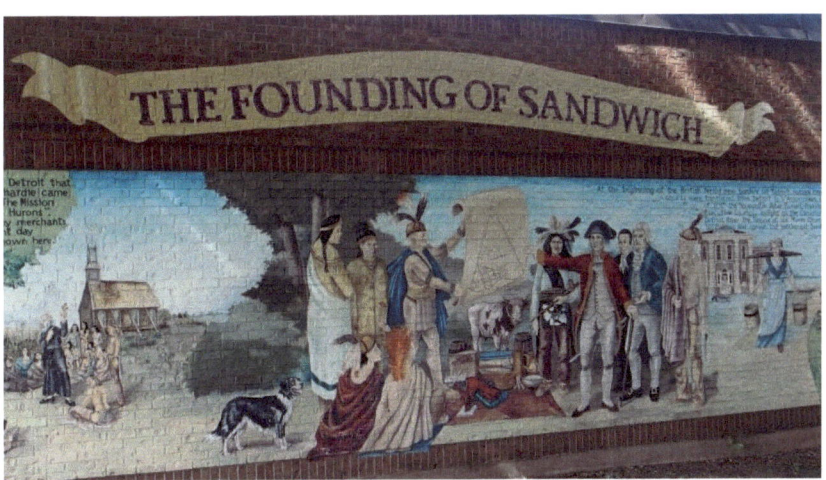

At the beginning of the British period, new borders set Detroit outside Canada and the courts were transferred from Detroit to L'Assomption. In the summer of 1797, the Honourable Peter Russell, President of the Executive Council, bought on the Canadian side of the Detroit River the reserve at the Huron Church containing 1,078 acres and named the settlement Sandwich.

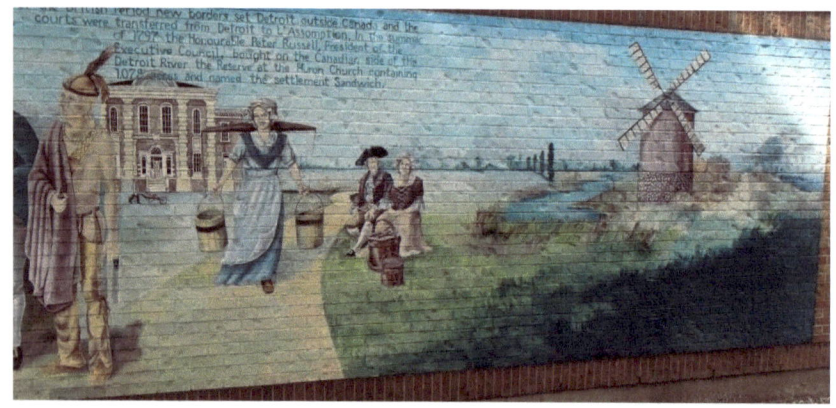

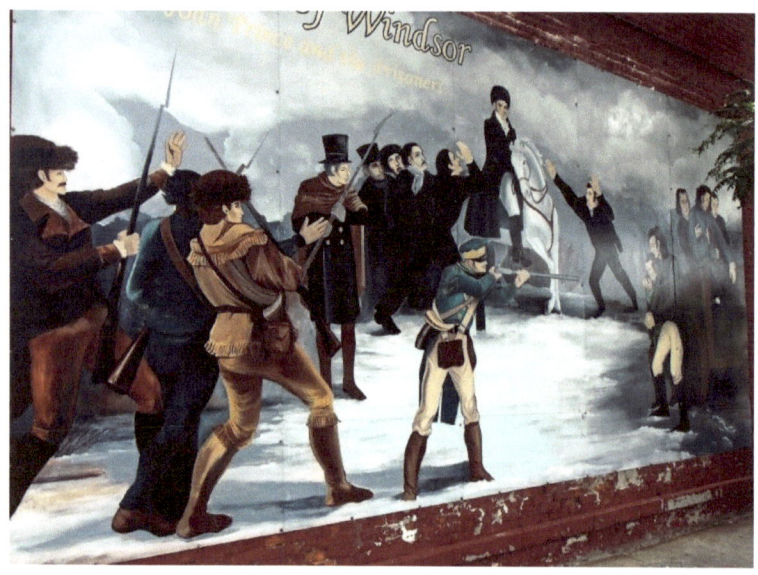

Battle of Windsor

On December 4, 1838, Colonel John Prince awoke at 6 a.m. by an alarm gun at Sandwich. He saw a fire at Windsor and proceeded there with the militia and found it in the possession of Brigands and Pirates. They attacked and killed 27 and took 20 prisoners, five of whom were ordered to be shot. After that, all prisoners were shot on the spot. Later in the day, several men including Reverend Johnson and Samuel James entreated Colonel Prince not to commit murder by shooting the prisoners but begged them to leave them to the laws of the country.

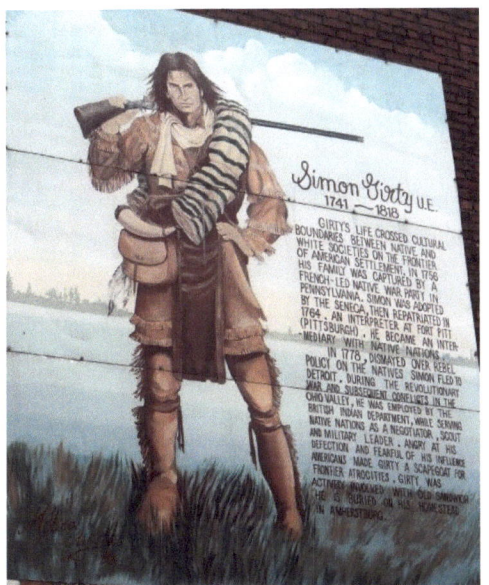

Simon Girty (1741-1818) – his life crossed cultural boundaries between Native and white societies on the frontier of American settlement. In 1756 his family was captured by a French-led native war party in Pennsylvania. Girty was adopted by the Seneca, then repatriated in 1764. An interpreter at Fort Pitt (Pittsburgh), he became an intermediary with native nations.

Architectural Terms

Brackets: a decorative or weight-bearing structural element which forms a right angle with one side against a wall and the other under a projecting surface such as an eave or roof. Example: 3203 Peter Street, see Page 32	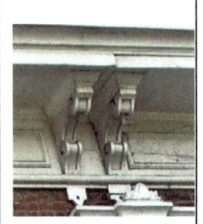
Buttress: a masonry structure built against or projecting from a wall which serves to support or reinforce the wall. In Canadian architecture, they are sometimes used for decoration. Example: Assumption University, see Page 30	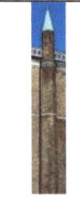
Capital: The uppermost finish or decoration on a column. A Corinthian column is characterized by a rounded capital decorated with acanthus leaves and a square abacus (the uppermost portion of a capital directly below the entablature) on tall slender columns. Example: Hiram Walker building, see Page 15 A Doric column is characterized by a plain column with no base, a shaft with twenty flutings, and a simple capital with a simple entablature. Example: 3255 Sandwich Street, see Page 41	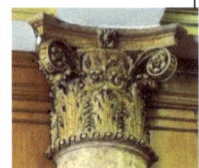 Corinthian 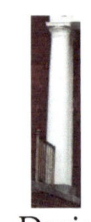 Doric

Cornice: originally the wooden overhang of the roof. With the use of stone, brick, iron and steel, the cornice is any projecting shelf at the top of a ceiling or roof. They can be very decorative. Example: 3203 Peter Street, see Page 32	
Cornice Return: decorative element on the end of a gable. Example: 3215 Peter Street, see Page 56	
Dentil Moulding: an even series of rectangles used as ornamental decoration in cornices. Example: 3255 Sandwich Street, see Page 41	
Dome: Any roof structure that is curved and spans an ultimately circular base. Squinches and pendentives are used to provide a circular base on a square or rectilinear tower. A squinch is a construction filling in the upper angles of a square room so as to form a base to receive an octagonal or spherical dome. When a square space is vaulted to provide a circular space for a dome the resulting curved triangular supports are called pendentives. This is most common in Byzantine architecture. Example: 2879 Riverside Drive East, Page 26	
Dormer: (French for "sleep") a gable end window that pierces through the plane of a sloping roof surface to create usable space in the top floor or attic of a building by adding headroom. Example: 3522 Sandwich Street, see Page 47	

Entrance: The entrance encompasses the doorway and the inner vestibule or, in residential architecture, the covered porch. Example: 3215 Peter Street, see Page 56	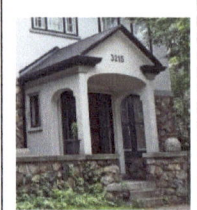
Gable: the triangular portion of a wall between the edges of a sloping roof. Example: 351 Mill Street, see Page 33	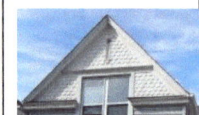
Hipped Roof: a roof where all sides slope downwards to the walls with no gables. Example: Sandwich Street, see Page 47	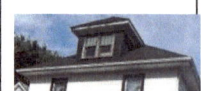
Keystones and Voussoirs: a voussoir is a wedge-shaped element used in building an arch. A keystone is the central stone that locks all the stones into position, allowing the arch to bear weight. A keystone is often enlarged and embellished. Example: 3203 Peter Street, Pg. 32	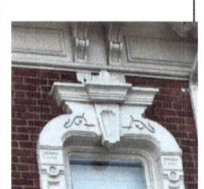
Lancet Window: a tall, narrow window with a pointed arch at its top. Example: Assumption University, see Page 31	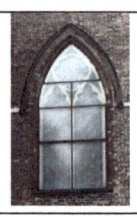

Pediment: a triangular section above the horizontal structure (entablature), typically supported by columns. The inside of the triangle is called the tympanum. Example: 3203 Peter Street, see Page 32	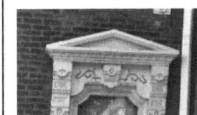
Rose Window: a circular window with ornamental tracery radiating from the centre. Example: Riverside Drive, Our Lady of the Rosary Church, see Page 26	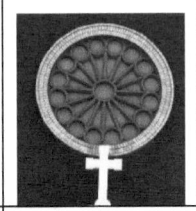
Sidelight: a window, usually with a vertical emphasis, that flanks a door, and is often used to emphasize the importance of a primary entrance. **Transom Window:** the light above the doorway, also called a fanlight. Example: 3255 Sandwich Street, see Page 41	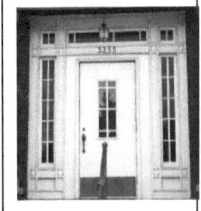
Window Hood: A **hood** is the piece found above window openings, usually of an ornate design, and covers the top third of the opening. Hoods are commonly placed above arched or curved openings on both windows and doors. Example: 3203 Peter Street	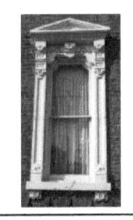

Florentine Renaissance, early 14th to early 16th centuries - places emphasis on symmetry, proportion, geometry and the regularity of parts; there us orderly arrangements of columns, pilasters and lintels, as well as the use of semicircular arches, hemispherical domes, niches and shrines. Italy of the 15th century, and the city of Florence in particular, was home to the new architectural style of Renaissance. Example: 2072 Riverside Drive East, Page 9	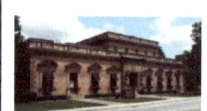
Georgian, before 1860 – This style began with the British King Georges in the 18th century. These buildings have balanced facades around a central door, medium-pitched gable roofs, and small paned windows. Example: 3255 Sandwich Street, see Page 41	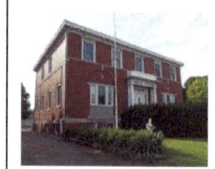
Gothic Revival, 1830-1890 – These decorative buildings have sharply-pitched gables with highly detailed verge boards, pointed-arch window openings, and dichromatic brickwork. It is a common style in Ontario. Example: 3243 Sandwich Street	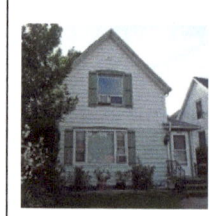
Italianate, 1850-1900 – It has wide-bracketed eaves, belvederes, wrap-around verandahs. Example: 3534 Sandwich Street, see Page 40	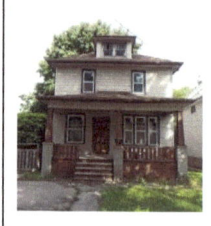

Renaissance Revival (1870 - 1910) - The Renaissance Palazzo was a three or four storey building with a rusticated (very large masonry blocks with deep joints and decorated with rough or bold finishes) ground floor, and regularized understated windows on two upper levels, always finished by an elaborate cornice. The Renaissance saw the development of a graceful and balanced adaptation of the Greek styles. In Ontario, the Renaissance was revived in commercial buildings, banks, offices, and churches in many towns. Most of the Renaissance Revival buildings are designed without columns while those with columns and pilasters are more ornate. Example: 3277 Sandwich Street – Mackenzie Hall, Sandwich, Page 43	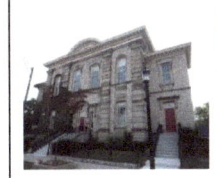
Romanesque Revival, 1880-1910 – This style hearkens back to medieval architecture of the 11th and 12th centuries with a heavy appearance, blocky towers and rounded arches. Example: 2879 Riverside Drive East, Page 26	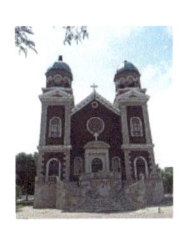

Vernacular/Traditional Mode 1638 - 1950 Influenced but not defined by a particular style, vernacular buildings are made from easily available materials and exhibit local design characteristics. Example: 412 Prince Street, see Page 52	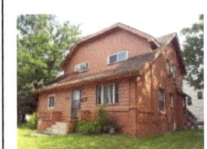
Victorian - In Ontario, a Victorian style building can be seen as any building built between 1840 and 1900 that doesn't fit into any of the other categories. It encompasses a large group of buildings constructed in brick, stone, and timber, using an eclectic mixture of Classical and Gothic motifs. Example: 3203 Peter Street, see Page 32	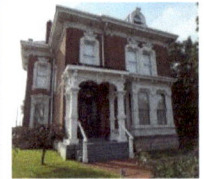

www.ingramcontent.com/pod-product-compliance
Lightning Source LLC
Chambersburg PA
CBHW040843180526
45159CB00001B/296